Chernobyl

Chernobyl
The Forbidden Truth

Alla Yaroshinskaya

Translated by Michèle Kahn and Julia Sallabank

Introduction by David R. Marples

Foreword by John Gofman

University of Nebraska Press
Lincoln

First published in English in 1994 by Jon Carpenter Publishing.

First translated from the Russian by Michèle Kahn for Editions de l'Aube,
France. Translated into English from the French by Julia Sallabank.

Photographs by M. Metzel.

♻ The paper in this book meets the minimum requirements of American
National Standard for Information Sciences—Permanence of Paper for Printed
Library Materials, ANSI Z39.48-1984.

Library of Congress Cataloging-in-Publication Data
Yaroshinskaya, Alla.
[Chernobyl', sovershenno sekretno. English]
Chernobyl, the forbidden truth / Alla Yaroshinskaya; translated by Michèle
Kahn and Julia Sallabank; introduction by David R. Marples; foreword by John
Gofman.
p. cm.
ISBN 0-8032-4912-8 (cloth: alk. paper).—ISBN 0-8032-9910-9 (pbk.: alk.
paper)
1. Chernobyl Nuclear Accident, Chornobyl', Ukraine, 1986. 2. Chernobyl
Nuclear Accident, Chornobyl', Ukraine, 1986—History—Sources. I. Title.
TK1362.U38Y3713 1995
363.17'99'0947714—dc20
95-2963 CIP

Contents

And the third angel sounded, and there fell a great star from heaven, burning as it were a lamp, and it fell upon the third part of the rivers, and upon the fountains of waters; and the name of the star is called Wormwood: and the third part of the waters became wormwood; and many men died of the waters, because they were made bitter.

Revelations 8

Chernobylnik: a variety of absinthe (wormwood) with a red-brown or deep purple stem.

S. Ozhegov, *Dictionary of the Russian Language*

List of illustrations

Chernobyl, 1989. The notice reads: 'The party of Lenin, the power of the people . . . will lead us to victory.'

Introduction

David R. Marples

The Chernobyl disaster of April 1986 has been the subject of numerous monographs, interpretations, and predictions as to its causes,
fallout, and ultimate health consequences. Yet rarely has it been per-
ceived within the perspectives of its time: that of the late Soviet
period, with the USSR having barely taken the first steps of glasnost,
and its new leader, Mikhail Gorbachev, clearly still consolidating his
power. For the leadership it was an unwelcome event, but one that
initially—it appeared—could be contained, dealt with internally, and
carefully concealed from the public eye. Once the radiation had
crossed the Soviet borders, however, and penetrated Sweden and
Central Europe, the Soviet authorities faced an unprecedented phenomenon: a major nuclear catastrophe that had elicited world attention and demanded a response.

At the same time, the consequences of the explosion were unknown. There was considerable speculation about the levels of radiation, the number of deaths, and the severity of other effects, as well
as questions about whether the graphite fire had been extinguished
and whether radiation was continuing to seep from the destroyed
reactor. What areas needed to be evacuated, and what levels of radiation were acceptable for human habitation? The few known examples
of similar events—Hiroshima and Nagasaki, accidents in space, leaks
from nuclear submarines, and the Three Mile Island nuclear plant
accident in the United States seven years earlier—were, for one reason or another, hardly comparable. Gorbachev and several Western

spokespersons focused on what Chernobyl told us about the dangers of nuclear war.

Over the next three years, the drama of Chernobyl unfolded. The damaged reactor was capped with a concrete shell that ostensibly would last "for eternity." The official number of victims remained static at thirty-one. The Soviet nuclear authorities worked closely with the International Atomic Energy Agency (IAEA), presenting an official report to the meeting in Vienna in August 1986 under the leadership of Valery Legasov, First Deputy Chairman of the Kurchatov Institute of Atomic Energy. The IAEA also began to examine Soviet nuclear reactors, particularly the Chernobyl-type graphite-moderated reactor (RBMK), and safety improvements were made to that reactor. Its shutdown time was reduced considerably, its uranium enrichment was increased, and measures were introduced to make it more difficult for anyone other than the director or chief engineer to dismantle safety mechanisms. The reactor nonetheless remained unstable when operated at low power. Once the 116,000 people living within a thirty-kilometer radius of the Chernobyl reactor had been evacuated, questions arose as to how this land might eventually be brought back into circulation. The Chernobyl plant itself was back in operation within five months.

Not everyone was satisfied with this apparent return to normalcy. Glasnost had generated some critical thinking on the nuclear as on other issues, particularly in the republics most affected by radiation fallout: Ukraine and Byelorussia. One of the focal points by the spring of 1989 was Narodichi, a small region to the west, with a town of the same name containing a population of about 9,500 and numerous small settlements. In theory, this region was outside the area of fallout. The population had taken no precautionary measures over the previous three years; indeed, many residents grew their own food on their small private plots of collective farms. Yet there were ominous signs of health problems, particularly among children, many of whom were experiencing thyroid problems. In Narodichi itself, one in every two school children was reportedly absent from school at any time due to illness.

Narodichi quickly became the focus of international and regional attention. Foreign scientists arrived in the region, along with various official Soviet scientific delegations. The area became the chief subject of a brief documentary film called *Mi-kro-fon!* Among those who had always doubted the official accounts of the consequences of Chernobyl was a Zhitomir newspaper reporter—shortly to become a deputy to the new Congress of People's Deputies of the USSR—Alla Yaroshinskaya. She had already authored or coauthored several articles expressing these doubts, one of which was published in *Moscow News* (a leader in the campaign for glasnost) with the heading, "The Big Lie." Under the circumstances, the reader might assume that the expression of such views in the late Gorbachev period was relatively easy, that Yaroshinskaya's views represented public feeling and the prevailing view of affairs. So they did. Yet her path was far from easy. Why should this be?

One reason was the continued authority and prestige of Soviet specialists, many of whom are described in this text: Yury Izrael, Leonid Ilin, Anatoly Romanenko, even Legasov until his suicide on the second anniversary of Chernobyl. Ilin's concept of a 35-rem safety limit for those affected by Chernobyl radiation was widely accepted by foreign specialists as below danger levels. As I discovered during an interview at the Center for Radiation Medicine in Kiev in 1989, virtually all the health problems could be dismissed as endemic to the particular regions: as they had always suffered from iodine deficiency in the soil, the population could be expected to experience thyroid problems. And if there were more health problems than before, this only indicated that the monitoring of health as a whole had improved, not that the population's overall health in the affected zone had worsened.

These specialists and others then turned with venom upon journalists. American journalists had from the first sensationalized the consequences of Chernobyl. Now, surely, Soviet journalists, unused to the freedoms of glasnost, were doing the same and more.

Radiophobia had penetrated the general population, which was now blaming radiation for every illness, no matter how minor. Yaroshinskaya found it difficult even to approach the microphone at the Congress when she wished to show the film *Zapredel* (Beyond the limit) to deputies. Journalists had never been highly regarded in Soviet life. Their function, after all, was to parrot party decrees and offer paeans to the General Secretary of the CC CPSU of the day. They were seen as a sycophantic and contemptible breed. A wide gap was demarcated between the "experts" and the journalists (often dismissed in the same breath, incidentally, with "Greens" or environmentalists) who were out to create sensations.

This elitist attitude has by no means been confined to the former Soviet Union. It has permeated a variety of scientific reports, dissertations, and monographs in the Western world. One, for example, has referred to Chernobyl as the "worst conceivable accident at a nuclear power plant," which at best can only be described as wishful thinking. One cannot examine Chernobyl adequately from the perspective of a single discipline, and those who attempt to do so are producing not definitive works but narrowly focused microcosms of the event.

Yaroshinskaya, however, always represented a new breed, tenacious and relentless. In those areas in which she is not a specialist, she has consulted experts and cited them at length. She has also reproduced the originally classified documents from the Third Department of the USSR Ministry of Health and other organizations. What she has described as a "cover-up" has become manifest: it indeed took place, and on a major scale. For three years, a vast population living under the impact of Chernobyl remained ignorant of that fact, eating contaminated food, tilling irradiated land, drinking milk and water that contained dangerous amounts of radionuclides. Cleanup workers, heavily affected by their work in the zone, returned to various far-flung parts of the USSR not embraced by the monitoring process. They will never be included in Chernobyl's casualty statistics, yet they will suffer, without compensation. Local party officials, for the most part, backed the official scientific expertise and hindered and harassed Yaroshinskaya at every opportunity.

Once she became part of the Soviet investigative team, however, she gained access to the secret Politburo documents that have revealed so much in this book. Shortly afterward, she began to publish the most relevant ones in the newspaper, *Izvestiya*. They reveal that the Soviet leaders, from Gorbachev downward, knew far more about the event than they revealed to the world, and that official statements were deliberately misleading and distorted. Perhaps the most shocking is the revelation that at the IAEA meeting in Vienna in August 1986, at which the Soviet delegation delivered an interpretation of the causes of the disaster, the authorities deleted, before the presentation of the report, a passage that named the faulty structure of the reactor's control rods as a prime cause of the accident. Also unpardonable was the failure to publicize the fact that more than 10,000 people were hospitalized less than two weeks after the explosion of 26 April 1986, or that some 1,500 of them were diagnosed as having radiation sickness.

One might ask at this juncture, as does Yaroshinskaya, who is to blame, and this book provides some answers to this question. But a subsidiary question might be: who is right? What is the correct interpretation of Chernobyl? The answer is not yet clear and has become muddled by western investigative teams. In the spring of 1991, shortly after the fifth anniversary of Chernobyl, the United Nations team of researchers, operating under the auspices of the International Atomic Energy Agency, issued a detailed report based on its researches into various villages in Ukraine and Byelorussia. It was not well received; it appeared to gloss over some of the key problems of Chernobyl, and it did not encompass either the cleanup crews or the evacuees. At this same time, new information was surfacing concerning health problems related to Chernobyl. This time, it would be very difficult for specialists to dismiss them as unrelated or not definitively related to Chernobyl.

In the spring of 1992, I attended the First International Chernobyl Congress, held in Minsk, Byelorussia, and listened to a variety of scientific reports. Among those that captured my attention was a presentation by Academician Evgeny Kanoplya, Director of the Institute of Radiobiology of the Byelorussian Academy of Sciences. Kanoplya revealed that more than 22 villages in Byelorussia were experiencing radiation levels above 40 curies per square kilometer of cesium in the soil. The clay soils of Byelorussia and northern Ukraine (Polessye) have been particularly receptive to radionuclides, which then rapidly penetrated the food chain.

How would this manifest itself in terms of health problems? There was as yet no evidence of an increase in leukemias, as Kanoplya acknowledged. The chief hematologist of the republic of Byelorussia could declare confidently in late 1992 that Chernobyl had not resulted in a massive rise in health problems for the republic, as the lack of rise in leukemias demonstrated. Earlier that same year, Ukrainian minister of health Yury Spizhenko was declaring that no one could definitively equate the disturbing rise in diseases among the Ukrainian population and the impact of Chernobyl radiation, but that Chernobyl must be considered one of many factors, the others encompassing an unhealthy lifestyle: heavy smoking, poor nutrition, the pollution of air and water by heavy industrial plants, and the like. The observer might have concluded that the ultimate health effects of Chernobyl, obscured by government secrecy and a whole host of unrelated factors, would never be known.

But how convincing were these statements? One answer has been provided by Evgeny Demidchik, director of the Thyroid Tumor Clinic within the Byelorussian Institute of Oncology. Demidchik has studied the problem of thyroid cancer among children since 1966, when it was such a rare disease that the discovery of 1 case per year was exceptional. Four years after Chernobyl, however, there were suddenly more than 50 cases, all among children born before or during the Chernobyl disaster. By December 1993, over 260 cases had been revealed. More than 60 percent of them were in the Gomel region, the most affected by Chernobyl. A significant number were found in the eastern Brest oblast, close to the town of Pinsk, another region known to have been severely contaminated. The northeastern oblast of Vitebsk, which lay outside the fallout zone for radioactive iodine, on the other hand, registered only 6 cases. This virtual epidemic of thyroid cancers among children—and the cancer is a highly aggressive one that metastasizes rapidly if undetected—has occurred precisely in the zones of highest fallout.

The thyroid tumors have resulted from the fallout of radioactive iodine, which has a half-life of only eight days. The health impact of other persistent radionuclides, particularly cesium-137 and strontium-90, is unknown. The Byelorussian Institute of Radiation Medicine has begun an investigation of 500 children affected by high cesium intake, but its scientists note that their conclusions at this stage can be no more than tentative. One branch of the institute is located in northern Byelorussia, close to the Ignalina nuclear plant with its Chernobyl-style reactors. The institute there is monitoring the impact of low-level radioactive fallout from the plant on the population in the vicinity. Yaroshinskaya shows that the number of people hospitalized from Chernobyl was thousands of times higher than reported officially by Soviet spokespersons. Ukrainian government reports have cited some 8,000 cleanup workers dead to date. More than 3 million citizens of the former Soviet Union live in areas affected by radiation, and the death toll has continued to rise.

The true medical consequences of Chernobyl thus lie ahead. But the governments in question are less able to deal with them than was the now-defunct Soviet Union. Key technical specialists have left Ukraine and Byelorussia—particularly Russian scientists and nuclear personnel who did not wish to take up citizenship in their newly independent states. Both Ukraine and Byelorussia were suffering deep economic crises; in late 1994, and the new president in the latter country, Aleksandr Lukashenka, has sown reluctance to take any new initiatives in moving the nation toward a market economy. Chernobyl might indeed threaten the future of these nations, but their populations are preoccupied with a day-to-day struggle for existence amid hyperinflation, fast-rising prices, an energy crisis, and a significant rise in crime. In the case of Ukraine, a new factor has also arisen: the demand for an immediate supply of energy for both household and industrial purposes.

Ukraine was the most heavily industrialized of the Soviet republics, particularly in the Donbass-Dnieper economic zone, with its metallurgical plants, steel foundries, and coal mines. This region has continued to be a heavy consumer of energy. In the 1980s, the Soviet planners anticipated that Ukraine's demand for nuclear energy would continue to rise, and that by the end of the century, nuclear power would account for about 60 percent of Ukraine's total electricity production (about twice the Soviet average). Chernobyl sparked a significant antinuclear and environmental movement that was successful in halting the ambitious nuclear program. In the post-Soviet era, however, the program has been revived. An independent Ukraine, its supporters assert, simply has no alternative to nuclear power. The price of Russian oil and gas has risen sharply and is well beyond the means of the Ukrainian budget.

The decision lies with the Ukrainian government, and the political future of Ukraine appears perilous. Efforts at economic reform are just beginning. Ukraine's currency is almost worthless, and the economic crisis has deepened. Further, its territorial integrity is threatened from various quarters. The Crimea, to which the Russian parliament has laid claim on separate occasions, has elected a separatist president who desires closer ties between the Crimea and Russia, and there is widespread disaffection for the Kiev government in the Donbass and western Ukraine. Although a former East Ukrainian industrial manager, Leonid Kuchma, was elected the new president of Ukraine in July 1994, he received little support in western Ukraine and faced his first coal-miners' strike in the Donbass coalfield after only three months in office.

Given these problems, the reader might ask, why is Yaroshinskaya's book so important at this juncture? Why should we return to the theme of Chernobyl years later, as the now-independent states struggle for mere existence? The reason is simple: This book illustrates, as no one has before, the extent to which the Soviet regime could mislead its own people, even directly imperiling their lives. There can be and should be no return to the past. Whatever the difficulties of the current post-Soviet regimes, a resort to some form of quasi-Stalinist structure is not the answer.

Moreover, Yaroshinskaya also shows that an individual can make a difference, that the struggle of dissidents and opponents of the Soviet system was not futile but was a direct factor in the collapse of the USSR in December 1991. Her contribution to knowledge is to elucidate the world's largest disaster in the sphere of nuclear energy. The Chernobyl story is far from over. Its effects have been exacerbated by misleading reports and the careful and systematic concealment of information on the victims' health. If the voice heard on these pages is a shrill one, the reader should recall that Yaroshinskaya herself experienced the ramifications of the tragedy; those suffering in Zhitomir are her neighbors and compatriots. Under the circumstances, hers could not be a dispassionate and detached voice. It is an angry one that demands to be heard.

Finally, the Western countries have an important role to play in the future of Ukraine, Byelorussia, and the other ex-Soviet states. At the least, they can provide expertise to ensure that, if nuclear energy must be pursued in the immediate future, reactors are as safe as possible. They must raise questions about the continuing operation of the unsafe reactors at Chernobyl, or the wisdom of having six reactors, each of 1,000 megawatts capacity, at a single station in the industrial and heavily populated region of Zaporozh'ye. And the West must also recognize the fragility of these governments and the problems that Chernobyl has brought them, and adopt an attitude of understanding and compassion. Our own problems remain minor by comparison.

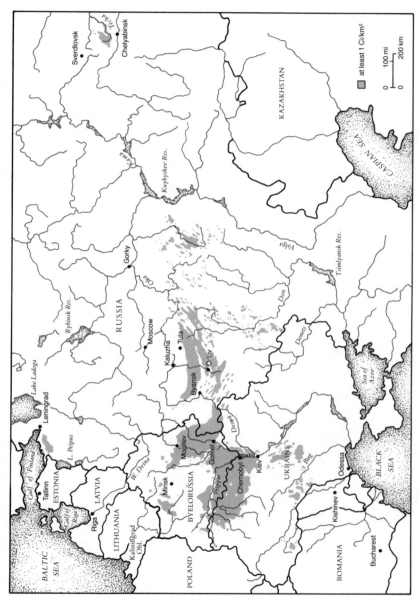

Overview of caesium-137 contamination in central Europe, early 1990s, showing areas with at least one curie of contamination per square kilometre. Highest levels of contamination are in the Ukraine and Byelorussia; see following maps.

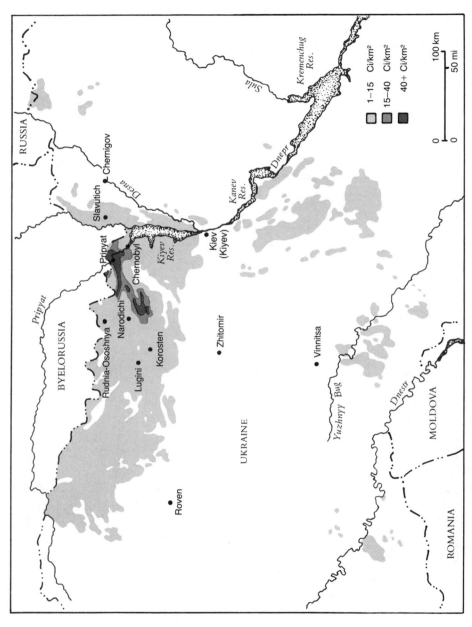

Levels of caesium–137 in Ukraine, 1991, in curies per square kilometre.

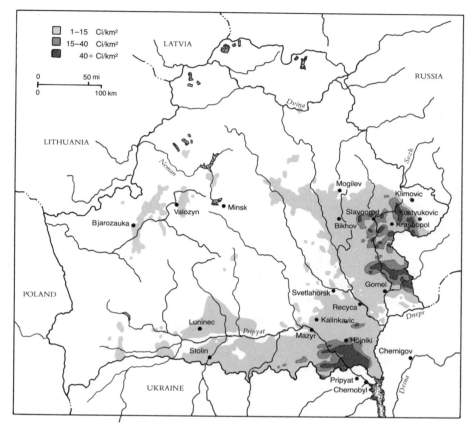

Levels of caesium-137 in Byelorussia, 1993, in curies per square kilometre.

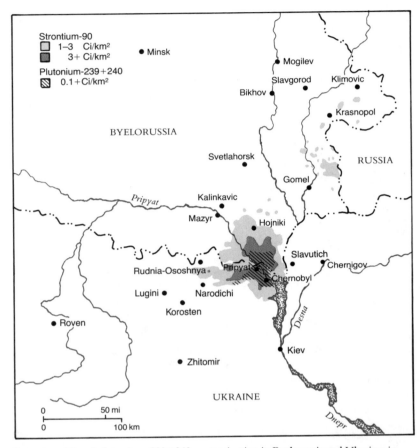

Strontium-90 and plutonium-239+240 contamination in Byelorussia and Ukraine, in curies per square kilometre. The levels for the two are combined in the map of Byelorussia.

Data for maps from *Radiation Contamination on Ukrainian Territory,* Moscow: Committee of Geodesy and Cartography of the USSR, 1991: *Rèspublika Belarus': Review-Topographic Map with the Data on Radiation Contamination* and *Map of Radiational Situation on European Part of Commonwealth of Independent States and the Baltic States for January 1993,* Minsk: BelCGE Belgeodesy, Committee of Geodesy under the Council of Ministers of the Republic of Belarus, 1993.

Foreword

by Professor John Gofman

IT may surprise the reader to hear my serious recommendation to all people who care about their personal health, their future health, their children's health, and the health of future generations—and, I might add very seriously, all who care about the ecology of our planet. That recommendation: Read and take very seriously the true meaning of Alla Yaroshinskaya's *Chernobyl: The Forbidden Truth*.

My research for the past thirty years has been in the evaluation of the health risks posed by ionizing radiation from nuclear activities associated with the 'peaceful' *and* the 'warlike' atom. My work is in 'hard science' evaluation of the health risks. Whatever my emotional commitments may be, my task in these endeavours necessarily is to produce a scientifically rigorous evaluation. Such an evaluation abhors exaggerations either in the direction of over-estimation or underestimation of the health risks of exposure to ionizing radiation—risks such as cancer and leukemia in this generation, and risks of these and numerous other diseases and impairments in many, many future generations. Indeed, the only source of self-esteem for my efforts can come from the extent to which my scientific evaluations prove to have been objective and validated by subsequent events.

Alla's path and mine crossed because of a momentous event, a crossroad for the health of humans for reasons to be elaborated below—the Chernobyl nuclear power plant accident in 1986. Within a few months of that accident, and based upon my past researches and Chernobyl-related measurements, I predicted at a major scientific meeting that the long-term consequences just for cancer and leukemia would be approximately 475,000 cancer deaths, plus an additional 475,000 non-fatal cancers. There is no reason to change that assessment today. But there has been a great deal of work needed to assess additional consequences, particularly concerning serious thyroid diseases as well as the inheritance of gene and chromosomal defects resulting from the worldwide radiation exposure. My most recent work in these endeavours will be published shortly in *Radiation and Chernobyl: This Generation and Beyond* (C.N.R. Books, PO Box 421993, San Francisco, Ca 94142).

Nuclear-committed governments would like to believe that there may be very few, if any, long-term effects of the Chernobyl accident.

Far, far away in Zhitomir, Ukraine, a very courageous woman journalist was beginning a journalistic endeavour fraught with personal danger (more from political chicanery than from personal radiation exposure). Much of that adventure is the substance of her present book. Until last year I had only read—with much interest—a translation of Alla's article, 'The Kremlin Sages' Forty Secret Protocols'. The total story being told here by Alla goes far beyond that.

In 1992 there was a very great surprise. Alla and I became co-recipients in Stockholm of one of the Right Livelihood Awards: she for her courageous and astonishing journalism concerning the abysmal handling by the Soviet government of the Chernobyl disaster (here described in detail), and I for my scientific work on health effects of radiation, including that done in evaluation of the health consequences of the Chernobyl accident.

I wish to say to the reader that Alla Yaroshinskaya has not only proven her outstanding capability as an investigative journalist and writer, but she impresses me indelibly as a charming human with exceptional qualities of compassion, of dedication to honesty, fairness and truth, and a person of great appreciation for the beauty of our natural world and loving concern for the children of the world.

Since our meeting in Stockholm we have been communicating extensively about our mutual concern that the full truth of the current and future health consequences from Chernobyl should be evaluated *and* communicated to the world public. And we are both concerned, for excellent reasons, at the fact that there has existed, and continues to exist, a massive and worldwide campaign to prevent that truth from becoming known.

Your health and your life may be at stake. The grounds for this concern are described below.

Biomedical un-knowledge and nuclear pollution

'Biomedical un-knowledge' is shorthand for all the findings which are the opposite of what is true about health and disease. The rational person would of course assume that no one wants biomedical un-knowledge. *Not so!* There is a market *eager* for medical un-knowledge in the field of health consequences from nuclear (and other) pollutants. There are financially and politically powerful interests who assume that they have a lot to lose if research finds that their pollutants are deadly. And in their short-sighted view, that assumption can be correct.

The market? Yaroshinskaya amply describes the Soviet market which operated in the post-Chernobyl era in grossly anti-human ways (while talking about the humanity of their socialist enterprises).

And the ex-USSR is not alone. Nuclear energy, whether the 'peaceful' or the 'military' atom, represents a dearly beloved project of governments in the United States, Britain, Russia, France, Germany and Japan—as well as India, China, Pakistan, Iran and a host of 'wannabees'. Nuclear energy is fiercely defended by governments, whatever party is currently in power. They all realise that their fiercest defence will fail if the public comes to realize that radiation is harmful, even at the lowest doses. In lavish sponsorship of scientists, engineers and physicians in innumerable institutions worldwide (including many halls of academe), the governments have a wish-list for the outcome of radiation research (into Chernobyl, for instance). The wish-list includes the following 'findings'. Note that I did not say that a 'finding' has any need to be true: it needs only to be saleable.

3

One   Best of all would be a finding that a little extra radiation improves human health. This is called 'hormesis', and its more avid proponents are now ready to treat society for Radiation Deficiency Disease.

Two   In case hormesis does not sell well to the public, the next best finding is that there exists a so-called threshold dose of radiation. For exposures below that mythical safe dose, repair mechanisms will take care of everything. Safe. Safe. Safe. Never mind mentioning the powerful evidence and logic which prove that no such safe dose exists for cancer or inheritable disorders.

Three   If hormesis and thresholds are not saleable to the public, there is always the retreat to the unproven position that slow delivery of radiation (as will be given to the public in accidents such as Chernobyl) is far less harmful than radiation delivered rapidly, as in nuclear war. (Even ten times less harmful.)

A warning

I, too, would prefer radiation to be harmless. Who would not?

But unfortunately evidence and logic do *not* support the wish-list. Low-dose ionizing radiation may well be the most important single cause of cancer, birth defects and genetic disorders. Adding to the unavoidable dose received from natural radiation sources will possibly be one of mankind's greatest follies. This is my view, which is a view independent of government sponsorship.

Surely it was no accident that governments sponsoring nuclear energy programmes also became the major—or virtually only—sponsors of research ostensibly dedicated to discovering the truth about health hazards from radiation exposure. In similar fashion it is reasonable to surmise that the tobacco industry would have liked to capture control of all the research on health hazards from smoking.

Alla Yaroshinskaya's description of the repression of scientists and physicians and the suppression of scientific information in the

4

former USSR provides blatant examples of what it means to have governments sponsoring nuclear research and health evaluation. Personal experience and observation show that the situation is not fundamentally different in other countries. Dissident scientists may experience loss of jobs and livelihood, without immediate loss of life itself.

The public is not without power to protect itself

In recent times, most governments have found that it is not wise to suggest, 'Let them eat cake.' Not all the current crop of politicians are enamoured of Marie Antoinette's fate. Deceit is far more successful—and the cost is relatively low. Government agencies have found that supporters can be hired to defend virtually any pollutant.

Not all medical science is corrupt. There is *not* always a special interest that would like to falsify the outcome of medical studies. Nonetheless, medical science long ago realized that false findings can either be planned, or can be the result of innocent self-deception. And to avoid endless hassling over the validity of results, some basic Rules of Research have evolved for studies of health effects of pollutants, of dietary manipulations, of efficacy of pharmaceuticals. If it is not absolutely clear that the fundamental Rules of Research have been followed meticulously, there is no need to accept either the database on which findings rest, or the findings themselves.

We shall list nine of the prominent Rules of Research. In one way or another, they are repeatedly listed in the medical science literature. No real scientist can claim not to have known the Rules of Research. Yet in many fields the Rules are violated. The health effects of radiation represent an area with some massive violations of the Rules, both in preparing the database for examination and in analyzing the findings themselves for biological meaning.

The key to believable biomedical research is obedience to the Rules of Research. It follows that the public can solve the problem of getting honest health information concerning radiation if it can figure out and ESTABLISH

5

a mechanism to ensure that the Rules of Research receive meticulous imple-
mentation, and not merely lip service. This is true for nuclear pollution,
such as from Chernobyl, and it is true for legions of other pollutants such
as dioxin, lead or mercury. The public has a crucial function in establishing
the mechanism, which will NOT *be provided to it from on high. Neither*
academe nor government can be relied upon to establish it, and there will
be powerful opposition to effective implementation of this mechanism, for
obvious reasons. I have proposed such a mechanism, and it follows the
Rules of Research below.

Nine essential rules of inquiry

Adherence to the following rules is essential for conducting scientifically credible studies of Chernobyl's radiation consequences,
short or long term. Specifically for the evaluation of a 'Chernobyl',
we are talking about comparing the fates of exposed and non-
exposed groups of persons.

• FIRST RULE: *Comparable groups.* An essential condition for
determination of radiation effects is the assurance that exposed and
non-exposed groups of persons would have the *same* rate of disease
and disorders in the absence of radiation.

• SECOND RULE: *A real difference in dose.* If the rate of disease is
being compared in two groups, it is essential to achieve a reasonable certainty that the compared groups have appreciably *different*
accumulated doses. If the compared groups in fact received *nearly*
the same total amount of radiation, it is predestined before the study
even begins that analysis will find 'no provable difference in disease
rates between the two groups'.

• THIRD RULE: *A sufficiently big difference in dose.* The dose-
differences between compared groups must be large enough to
allow for statistically conclusive findings, despite the random vari-
ations in numbers and in population samples. Analysts can cope
with the random fluctuations of small numbers both by assuring

sufficiently large dose-differences between compared groups, and by assuring large numbers of people in each group.

• FOURTH RULE: *Careful reconstruction of dose*. Obviously, false conclusions will be drawn if supposedly *non-exposed* people in a database really received appreciable doses, and supposedly high-dose people received lower doses than the database indicates. The non-uniform nature of the Chernobyl releases of radioactivity makes this scientific pitfall into a real possibility, unless careful and objective dose reconstruction is substituted for assumptions. It is virtually imperative to use biological dosimetry here, since the physical dosimetry will not be truly a reliable indicator of dose received. (Biological dosimetry measures something in the person, such as chromosome injuries, which are produced in proportion to total dose received. It avoids all the arguments as to whether the measurements in the field tell the true exposure.)

• FIFTH RULE: *'Blinding' of dose analysts*. In a valid study of health response to a particular radiation dose, the analysts who estimate doses must have no idea of the medical status of the individual or group on which they are working. The health status and dose-related data must never be present in the same file. In other words, dose analysts must do their work blind, in order to protect the database from a wish-list answer about the relationship between dose and health.

• SIXTH RULE: *'Blinding' of diagnostic analysts*. In order to achieve scientific credibility, studies must show proof of precautions against bias not only in the dose-input, but also in the health-response output. In a valid Chernobyl study, the principle of blinding must extend to all analysts, physicians and technicians who diagnose the health status of persons in the study. They must *not* know whether a person's radiation dose was high or low, and they must be denied information (such as place of residence) which would allow them to form a personal opinion about the

7

likely dose. Crucial is the requirement that teams of 'special experts' have no ability to alter diagnoses later—unblinded.

• SEVENTH RULE: *No changes of input after any results are known.* One of the fundamental rules in an ongoing study is that no one is allowed to make retroactive alterations, deletions or additions to input-data after any of the health-response results are known. If there is an opportunity for health results to influence a study's revised input, there is clearly an opportunity to falsify the real cause-effect relationships (if any) between dose and response. A study becomes properly suspect if retroactive changes have been made in diagnosis or dose; if cases have been shuffled into new groupings (cohorts); if any data or cases have been suddenly dropped from the study; or if new cases have suddenly been added 'as needed' from some reserve.

• EIGHTH RULE: *No excessive subdivision of data.* It is in the nature of numbers that even the largest databases can be rendered inconclusive and misleading if analysts keep the data subdivided into too many categories or subsets. Therefore, subdivision must be watched with a degree of suspicion.

Inconclusive results: if analysts hope a study will find no provable effects, this result can be arranged by creating a 'small numbers problem', which will prevent almost all results from passing the test of statistical significance.

Misleading results: preservation of excessive subdivision also increases the frequency of finding a few effects at random which do pass the test of statistical significance, but which are nonetheless unreal (false).

• NINTH RULE: *No prejudgements.* Prejudgements are seldom compatible with objective inquiry.

Violations of the Rules of Research

The Rules of Research have been massively violated in essentially all epidemiological studies of health effects of radiation. Many, many studies in the literature fail to meet most of the Rules. The Hiroshima-Nagasaki studies have been justifiably criticized on these grounds, and, with possible rare exceptions, studies thus far into the effects of the Chernobyl accident have failed to meet the Rules.

The Rules are well known to the nuclear-committed governments, so they know fully how one can violate them. The Rules can certainly be violated repeatedly in the future. The result could be the creation of Biomedical Un-knowledge that will fill the textbooks of medicine for the next hundred years. What is true about radiation and health would be labelled untrue: what is untrue would become prevailing wisdom.

What would it take to be able to commit such a human injustice? THE ESSENTIAL REQUIREMENT IS TOTAL CONTROL OVER THE INPUT TO THE DATA-BASE, THE PROCESSING OF THE DATA, AND THEIR ANALYSES. In fact, control over input and output data themselves (dose and clinical findings) can suffice to predetermine the 'findings' of all users of the database. Once a database is 'managed', even the most innocent analyst will contribute to a flood of Biomedical Un-knowledge.

The effort by nuclear-committed governments to keep control over every significant radiation database continues in full force.

The central Chernobyl database is already under construction by the International Program on Health Effects of the Chernobyl Accident (IPHECA/WHO). Arrangements have been made with the governments of Russia, Byelorussia and the Ukraine to permit this. The main sponsors of the IPHECA study are the governments of the United States, Britain, France, Germany, Japan and Russia.

Is it possible that these studies will be honestly done? The answer to this question is, 'Yes, it *is* possible.' *But that is exactly the*

9

wrong question. Ask yourself if you would permit the tobacco industry to control all the studies of the health effects of cigarette smoking?

It is *totally unacceptable*—and unnecessary—that key radiation studies be conducted under circumstances that can either totally compromise the studies, or permit their use to produce un-knowledge. This warning in no way impugns the motives or work of some of the scientists who analyze such data. We *must* reiterate: if the Rules of Research are violated in handling a database, no analysis of such data can escape the poison. The first obligation of every objective scientist is to question the believability of raw data *before* he or she uses them, and at the very least to discuss the issue whenever questionable databases are used.

The need for a scientific watchdog

Since the key to believable biomedical research is obedience to the Rules of Research, it follows that citizens must propose and establish a specific mechanism to ensure scrupulous compliance with those Rules. It is proposed here to begin with the Chernobyl database.

I propose that a team of *independent* 'watchdog' scientists be established to work inside IPHECA's Chernobyl study with the authority (a) to check that every Rule of Research is obeyed, (b) to blow the whistle publicly if there are questionable practices, and (c) to publish its own views as an integral part of every IPHECA document. Such a watchdog authority cannot be temporary. Although preparation of the database is most intense at the beginning of a project, input is necessarily added to the database for many, many decades, as the health of the participants is followed up. Moreover, experience with the 1986 handling of the Hiroshima-Nagasaki database demonstrates that the most massive rule violations may occur in a long term study even decades after its inception.

The watchdog authority is a common sense proposal because it amounts to establishing a system which rewards and honours truth-telling, instead of punishing it by loss of employment or worse—which is what happens so often nowadays in every field from science to manufacturing or journalism. Alla Yaroshinskaya is an example of the wrong way one society (the former USSR) 'honoured' a truth-teller.

It is common sense for society to figure out how to reward the kind of behaviour it wants, instead of rewarding bad behaviour. The Right Livelihood Award deserves praise for recognizing this principle in what it honours. Jacob von Uexkull summarized the situation elegantly when he wrote: 'If our most important needs today are not new technological fixes but new social values and institutions […] then these priorities need to be reflected in what our society honours and supports.'

Setting up the watchdogs

Step One: All of us urgently need to encourage people in Byelorussia, Ukraine, Russia and elsewhere to learn what the Rules of Research are all about, why they are not just an academic issue, and how they connect directly with a top concern of non-academic people everywhere: health. Health for themselves, their children and their grandchildren. The public, the press and other professions will not demand compliance with these Rules unless they are aware of them and aware of the potential mega-misery consequences of not insisting on scrupulous compliance.

Step Two: We need to establish the principle that any database under accumulation—for example, the IPHECA database concerning Chernobyl—is automatically provided with an independent and enduring watchdog authority.

But the task is certainly *not* to dictate a uniform analysis of data. That would be the opposite of good science. *The purpose of a watchdog is to ensure that the database itself can be trusted, and that dissent is not punished and not silenced.* Thus the sponsor of a database—IPHECA for example—would be required to include commentary and analysis from the watchdog authority in each of its publications.

11

Step Three: After the watchdogs are in place, people at the grass-roots must stay vigilant, decade after decade, to ensure that the independent experts do not become just sheep who wear a watchdog costume. One must remain realistic about human corruptibility.

Step Four: At the grassroots level, we must insist on two things.

(a) The watchdog must be adequately funded. The cost per database will not be trivial. But there is a simple criterion to use. If a database is worth having, then it is essential that it produce knowledge, not un-knowledge. Thus, if there is to be funding for an IPHECA, surely it would be reasonable that the independent watchdog have 5% of the budget that is provided by the sponsors of IPHECA itself. Indeed, sincerity on the part of those sponsoring IPHECA would itself seem to demand that funding be offered forthwith.

(b) The watchdog must have full, immediate and ongoing (for decades) access to protocols, tapes, documents, laboratory results, vital statistics—all the information about how the input to the database is generated. Input includes the medical and health observations, the ecological observations, the laboratory procedures and tests, the dose-estimates, and the methods of dose-reconstruction. All such items are part of the database.

Channelling the anger

As you read this book, you will experience anger—anger that humans should have been subjected to the treatment described by Alla Yaroshinskaya. She has performed a great service to humanity by containing her anger and patiently telling all of us just what has happened, and what can happen. One of her memorable statements will have a long life. For those not familiar with the periodic table of chemistry, let me say that Cs-137 is a description of the isotope of the element caesium with mass number 137. Pu-239 is a description of the isotope of the element plutonium with mass number 239. The accident occurred in 1986. Alla Yaroshinskaya writes in this book:

'Reading through these unique documents, it occurred to me that the most dangerous isotope to escape from the mouth of the reactor did not appear on the periodic table. It was Lie-86. A lie as global as the disaster itself.'

It is my fervent hope that the grassroots public will channel its anger too, and join the effort to set up the necessary safeguards (such as the watchdog authority described above). We can thereby help to prevent future human injustices, like those Alla so poignantly describes. We all owe that much to forthcoming generations of children.

JOHN W. GOFMAN, MD, PhD
Professor Emeritus, Molecular and Cell Biology
University of California at Berkeley

Everyday conversation in Chernobyl. The sign reads: 'Radioactivity'.

ONE

From peace to panic

M Y family lives in Zhitomir, a small forest town in the Ukraine. It's a very old Slavic land, where the first traces of human presence date from as long ago as two thousand BC. My ancestors tilled this land in the bronze age, and at the beginning of the iron age. As witnesses we have tombs and the remains of an ancient Russian town.

Zhitomir was first mentioned in the Chronicles in 1392. It is said that the town was named after its founder, a warrior under the Russian princes Alexander and Dir. The name is formed from two words, *zhito* and *mir*, which in Ukrainian mean 'rye' and 'peace'. Thus the town's name encapsulates a whole philosophy of life, which all people can understand.

At the centre of the town is the Castle Mount. According to tradition, this is where the town began. On this hill, bathed on one side by the waters of the River Kamianka, and on the other by the River Teterev, a fort was built. The town grew beside it, inhabited by artisans, blacksmiths, potters, hunters, farmers and merchants. The thick forests which surrounded Zhitomir were rich in game, wild fruits, mushrooms and edible roots. The rivers on whose steep banks the town was built teemed with fish. With a mysterious, infallible talent, our ancestors chose the most enchanting places to build their towns and temples. For eternity.

The surrounding area has kept its beauty; every walk reveals new marvels. Just a few kilometres from Zhitomir, you find your-self in the heart of virgin countryside: the Teterev, whose clear waters flow between enormous blocks of stone, the forest on both banks, the rocks covered with moss and trees, the gorges, and in the distance, among the tips of the dark green fir trees, the clear blue cupolas of a small village church. A lump comes to your throat, your heart overflows with a mysterious feeling of oneness with the forest, the river, and the church whose cross shines so brilliantly in the sunshine.

These, at any rate, were the thoughts that passed through my head on that day, 25 April 1986, as I walked through the woods with my family. It was springtime. A sense of freedom and renewal was in the air. The trembling blue petals of the crocuses were pushing up through last year's withered leaves. My two-year-old son, Sasha, knelt down by each flower to contemplate it.

We did not know—no-one yet knew—that a few hours later something would happen which would transform for ever this ancient wonderland, this forest, these fields and meadows, our whole lives. And that from now on, life on earth would not only be divided into epochs and eras, civilisations, religions and political systems, but also into 'before' and 'after' Chernobyl. The earth would never be the same as it had been before 26 April 1986 at twenty-four minutes past one ...

Zhitomir is 130 km from Kiev, the capital of the Ukraine. My husband and I sometimes spend an evening at the theatre there. We generally come straight home after the show, arriving back between midnight and one o'clock.

By a twist of fate, on 27 April, suspecting nothing—neither the radio, the television, nor the newspapers had mentioned the explosion which had happened at the Chernobyl nuclear reactor—we went to Kiev. The Japanese group 'Setiku' were performing that evening at the Ukrainian Palace of Culture. We left our car in an adjoining parking lot. I remember that the show was something quite special. It was great art: I can still see the all-white costumes of the players, the grace of their movements.

We left late in the evening, in an excellent mood. The road from Kiev to Zhitomir was drowned in the blossoming spring forests. Halfway home, we stopped and got out of the car to breathe the intoxicating greenness. Everything was silent. Cold stars glittered. On one side we could see quite clearly the Great Bear, like a ladle. The moon lit up everything clearly. We could almost hear the buds bursting on the trees next to us.

ALTHOUGH no official information about the Chernobyl reactor had been provided by the official Soviet media, in the neighbouring towns of Kiev, Zhitomir and Chernigov panic grew daily. No-one knew exactly what had happened, and the rumours were getting wilder and wilder. Iodine disappeared from chemists' shops. Many people thought that it could protect you from radiation, and they drank it neat, burning their throats and digestive tracts. The official medical services were silent. Eventually, after ten days, the Ukrainian Minister of Health, A. Romanyenko, gave us this precious advice: shut your windows and wipe your shoes carefully with a damp rag before entering a house. Wipe floors and furniture with a damp duster. These were all the precautions we were to take against the radioactivity.

It was from foreign radio broadcasts that we learnt that Block number 4 of the Chernobyl power station had blown up and that the radiation level had risen. Our official media only made the announcement two days later.

The joyful May Day festival was approaching and nobody would have believed that something terrible and ineradicable had happened. On 1 May, at Zhitomir, Kiev, Chernigov, in all the towns and villages of Ukraine, Byelorussia, Russia, the Baltic lands, all over the country, as in previous years, millions of people lined the streets. It was extremely hot. Not just mild, but hot. Children dressed in national costume, breathing radioactive fumes, danced on the Kreshchatik, the main street of the Ukrainian capital. On the stand, greeting the crowds, stood the members of the Ukrainian Politburo, government ministers, and invited guests. At almost precisely the same moment, senior civil servants were hurrying their children to Borispol airport to get them away from the scene of the catastrophe. The children of the betrayed workers and intellectuals were left behind to delight the eyes of the ministers; this was the price paid to give international opinion the illusion that all was well.

My friend Nina Smykovskaya, a journalist whom I had known since university days, and whom God had at last blessed with children at the age of forty, was not able to leave for her family home in Odessa until 7 May. By then panic had swept through Kiev. Nina went into labour early, at seven months, and gave birth to twins. She named them after the women who helped her in those terrible hours, Diana and Inna. The babies were weak and anaemic; their mother, not suspecting any danger, fed them for two weeks on milk which was full of iodine and radioactive caesium. When they were two months old, the doctors ordered an emergency total blood transfusion. The children were saved, but to this day one of them, Diana, has developed more slowly than the other. Nina explained to me that one had been injected with fresh blood, and the other with older, preserved blood. Now when they celebrate their birthday, it is the anniversary of the tragedy. Their life is difficult: their parents, both journalists, only have a tiny apartment. When I stay the night with them in Kiev, Victor has to sleep in the tiny kitchen while I have his bed-settee.

I remember very well the beginning of May that fateful year. A blue sky. Snowy white clouds. Heat. It was strange. Rumours were all around us. After the first of May they began to snowball. The radio and newspapers told us one thing, then people coming from the worst hit areas told us another. All seats on trains and planes leaving Kiev were booked up for months ahead. People were at their wit's end, terrified by the unknown, and were storming the trains. They wanted to go away, anywhere, as far as possible from Chernobyl.

I was no exception. My husband Alexander is a fireman, and some of his colleagues had been sent to Chernobyl to pump water under the destroyed reactor. On 7 May he telephoned me from work to try and persuade me to leave with the children. Easy to say—but where could we go? At that time I was working on the 'Industry and construction' column of the local Party newspaper *Radianska Zhitomirshchina*.

I put in a request for leave with the editor-in-chief. My section head made it a condition that before I went, I finished a paper on the construction of a factory at Krochna. The next morning the

The Chernobyl nuclear plant in September 1991.

paper was on his desk. It began with a sentence about the blossoming flowers around Zhitomir, and the wonderful scent of apples which wafted over the factory from the neighbouring gardens ...

We were not able to get seats on the flight to Armavir, a small town in the northern Caucasus where we had relatives. There were no more tickets to be had, not to Armavir, nor to any other destination. We only just managed to get seats on a train to Moscow, to stay with friends.

The scene at Zhitomir station resembled an Exodus. My eldest son, Milan, who was then in the fifth grade [Year 7], was unable to complete his last term at school. All parents who were able had been given permission to take their children out of school before the end of the school year.

The whole family came to the station: my mother, my husband's parents, my sister. We all held back our tears. The grandmothers joked with little Sasha and gave him cakes, sweets,

19

apples, toys. I was showered with advice and Milan, the eldest, was made to promise to be good and help me during the journey. It is eighteen hours by train from Zhitomir to Moscow. It was my youngest son's second birthday. We spent it on the train, surrounded by people just like ourselves, exhausted, overcome by misfortune.

We had no family in Moscow and I had rarely had any reason to go there. I had been once when I was in my third year at university, and a second time for work to report on the Exhibition of Achievements of the National Economy. The first time, I had seen nothing of the town, because I was thinking about a man I was in love with who was not there. The second time, Moscow had won my heart with its churches and little streets with pretty old names. For me, this is what makes all the charm of the capital.

This time, we were in no mood for sightseeing. We were met at the station by some Jewish friends of ours, Fayina Alexandrovna and her son Misha, who had used to live in Zhitomir, and who still spent their holidays there as they had inherited a house in the district. Misha was a student.

When we arrived at their house, the first thing we did was to take off all our clothes and wash them straight away. I did not know what level of radioactivity they might contain, but I was instinctively aware of danger.

I am grateful to these people who took us in, as I know that some people who had fled from the radiation found themselves ostracised in the places they fled to; other people thought them contagious.

We stayed with these friends for several days. They lived in a small flat in one of those poor-quality houses built in a hurry in the Kruschev era, and I could see that we were in the way. I managed to get tickets to Armavir. My cousins were waiting for us there, and we arrived on 14 May after an exhausting, twenty-four hour journey by train from Moscow-Adler.

The weather there was already hot. The first cherries were being picked. The garden was fragrant. Everything was calm, no-one talked much about Chernobyl; it was as if they were not

20

affected. (Three years later, I was to learn that the area of Krasnodar had also been contaminated by radiation.)

The first thing I did was to take the children to the local radiological station. The level of radioactivity on their clothes was normal for the region: 0.025 milliroentgens. At home, before Chernobyl, it was 0.017. They explained that the difference was due to the nearby Caucasus.

Despite the flowers and the heat, we did not find peace in Armavir. My youngest son fell ill. We saw a local doctor, a woman, who was all the more attentive when she learned that we came from the Ukraine. That might not seem extraordinary, but knowing Soviet medicine, we were especially grateful. Sasha was suffering from a sore throat and bronchitis together.

By the time he was better, my leave was up, and in June we had to go back to Zhitomir. The news from there was more or less reassuring. I could not leave the children in the Caucasus, there was no-one to look after them. I had to go back to work—I could not leave it—a Soviet family cannot live on just one salary.

A torrid summer awaited us. *Pravda* administered daily tranquillisers by the million in the form of soothing articles. I am still ashamed of the titles of some of my colleagues' articles: 'The song of the nightingales above Pripyat', 'Small mementos of the reactor', etc. These 'mementos' cost the health of millions of people in the region. But more of that later.

It seems to me that all through the summer of 1986, not one drop of rain fell on the town. The sky was a uniform pale blue, faded by the pitiless sun. The reactor had at last been sealed, after an incredible amount of sand, lead and other materials had been poured into it. Its 'funeral' was celebrated. Relatives wept over the lead coffins of the victims of the radiation. The engineers from the power station were sentenced. Was it all over? No, it had only just started. It was only three or four years after the catastrophe that we began to realise its extent, its fatal nature, and to perceive the truth about our sick society. The bell is tolling. Will we be able to hear it in the primitive depths of our communist cavern, deafened as we are by the ideology of self-satisfaction?

TWO

Rudnia-Ososhnya: zone of lies

As I have already said, at that time I was working on the newspaper *Radianska Zhitomirchtchina*. We learnt that four villages in the nearby district of Narodichi had been evacuated because of the lethal level of radiation prevalent there. According to the media (among them our paper), the inhabitants had been evacuated to safe zones where everything had been provided for them. There was nothing to make me think that anything odd was going on. It was only a hunch—perhaps it's a characteristic of journalists. What probably aroused my suspicions was the fact that the houses for the evacuees were being built in the immediate vicinity of Chernobyl, right next to the forbidden zone.

I decided to go and have a closer look. To be sure, our newspaper said that workers from all over the area were working there flat out, that the houses would be of high quality, but the choice of site was not explained. Was it really safe?

When I expressed my doubts to the editor-in-chief, he listened to me and then replied shortly that it was none of our business. I asked to be allowed to do a report on Narodichi district. Instead, I was sent to the district of Malino to prepare an article on technical progress in an experimental factory. I finished the article and still managed to go to Rudnia-Ososhnya in Narodichi, where the builders who had built the Malino factory were building a nursery school.

An old bus was put at my disposal, and after a ten-hour journey on a bumpy road, we arrived at the 'scene of the inquiry'. It was the end of the 1987 heatwave. The bus drove through lush forests where all kinds of birds were singing, we were practically running over mushrooms. The sunlight filtered through the canopy of trees. The driver, a middle-aged man, spoke sadly of the damage caused by Chernobyl to the land, to the wonderful mushroom-picking spots in the area. They were still there, oh yes, but it was forbidden to go into the forest, to sit on the ground, or to pick strawberries, blackberries, or mushrooms. Everything was poisoned. The local people, who did not understand the danger, still defied the ban and picked the mushrooms, either eating them themselves or selling them at the local market.

Rudnia-Ososhnya is a typical forest village. In the spring, when the gardens are in bloom, they look like a great carpet of flowers in the middle of a pine forest. Some builders were working on the edge of the forest; from what we were told, they were building communal baths. They were not very talkative and it started to rain. However, I still wanted to understand what was happening, why they were building it there, and what the level of radioactivity was.

At last they talked. If they were building baths, they said, it was precisely because of the high level of radioactivity. What the level was, they did not know: 'Some soldiers come here and take measurements, but they don't say anything.' The work was dragging on and on, although at first they had been told that everything should be finished in two months. But it was always the same, there was no crane. Why were communal baths for ten people needed on the edge of the village, when each family had their own? No-one knew.

The eight builders who were building the nursery school next door were more talkative. The oldest, Yuri Grishchenko, told us that the school would be very expensive for the State, that they had been there for more than a month and that the locals were beginning to make fun of them. They were asking what this school was for, when there were hardly any small children in Rudnia-Ososhnya, and the building could hold twenty-five.

That was the first time I heard the terrible words 'coffin allowance'. This was the term used for the thirty miserable extra roubles given to the local people and those working on the construction sites on top of their usual monthly allowance. That made one extra rouble a day. They ate split peas, noodles and beef. They could not afford chicken, they said, because the three roubles a day they were allowed for food would not cover it.

The builders complained of headaches and tiredness, which they blamed on the high levels of radiation.

Today, four years after the Chernobyl disaster, I can confirm that they were right. The village with the funny name of Rudnia-Ososhnya is now being evacuated. It has been declared unsafe for human habitation. But it is only now, four years later, that we have learned it officially. At the time, I had to keep my visit a secret from my employers.

After I had talked to the builders, we went to the other end of the village to look for the team leader's house. There was no local soviet [council], nor any officials from the collective farm. Rudnia-Ososhnya was a village 'with no future', just like ten thousand others in the country, forgotten by God and Soviet power, where all able-bodied people are grouped together in one team. In some of them there is no shop or post office, nor even a telephone or any other sign of civilisation. And yet there are people living there. They have needs like anyone else: for bread, clothes, matches, light, books, radio; and they cannot get hold of them. Today the government condemns the old policies which simply designated entire areas as 'without a future'. But they have missed the boat. The villages are dying. Perfectly good houses are boarded up, the pathways and cemeteries are overgrown with weeds. The people have got nearer to civilisation by leaving for the towns.

This is what Valentina Uchapovskaya, the team leader and a district member of the soviet, told me: 'There are ninety homes in our village. It's been put under special control. At Rudnia-Ososhnya we have twenty-seven children aged six to fourteen, two aged fifteen and sixteen, and six pre-school children. The primary school has been closed because the level of radiation there was 1.5 milliroentgens. It had thirteen pupils, and there are only

24

two classrooms. And now [this conversation took place at the end of summer 1987] the level of radiation in the water was 0.2 milliroentgens and 0.4 in the earth. A little bit more at one end of the village than at the other. I take measurements myself, but my counter is wrong,' said the team leader part ironically, part bitterly. 'In fact, the level is three times as high. Specialists came last year and measured 1.1 milliroentgens. They told us, "It won't kill you." The district soviet gave me the meter. Soldiers also come and take measurements, but they don't explain anything.

'You saw how they are building us a new nursery school. We wonder why. Well, it could be useful eventually. We have a lot of young men here, and not enough girls; we can use it as an old folks' home when they get old.

'And then we don't have any roads. You can't go from Rudnia-Ososhnya to Malye Minki by car. I talked about that at the Narodichi district council session. Roads and children. For the last ten years they've had to walk ten kilometres to get to school. After the radiation [that's how she said it: "after the radiation"], it wasn't practicable to walk on the road. They've been promising to mend it for six years now. True, they have asphalted the roads in the village. We wrote to Masol [chair of the Council of Ministers of the Ukraine]. After that, a civil servant from the regional Executive Committee came here and promised that the road would be resurfaced in just over a year.' It is truly said that we live in hope …

'They explained to us what had to be done, what we should eat, when we had already swallowed the whole periodic table,' continued the team leader, wiping her muddy hands on the hem of her dress. When we arrived, she was just digging up potatoes in her garden. Not far away, other women were doing the same. Children were playing in the sand next to them. A little farther away, a bonfire was being lit, and radioactive ash was falling onto the gardens, the vegetable patches, and the children's heads.

There had been talk, right after the accident, of removing a layer of soil all around the village. But there had obviously been a change of plan, and the area had simply been ploughed. The

25

village had been 'washed', but it was not until autumn 1987 that preparations were made to de-activate it using lime.

During that time, dozens of the village residents—who, apart from the first big bout of radiation, had been subjected to radiation for nearly three months after the accident, and had drunk radioactive milk—had ended up in the regional hospital. Some of them had been in twice.

The women working in their gardens came up to us. Hearing what we were talking about, they joined in, telling us of their sad everyday life. They told us that sixty-three cows had been taken to the Shchors kolkhoz [collective farm] in Bazar, another village in the district. They had been paid 1.92 roubles per kilo compensation. (It is only now, four years later, that it has been learned that the village of Bazar is to be completely evacuated.) Why to Bazar? We were told that it was a 'clean' place and that they could be fattened up for meat there. The cows were taken away on 17 July 1986. At first the heifers were left, but in the end these were taken too, two months before I arrived. The villagers were only allowed to keep pigs and chickens.

'In the first days after the explosion, we all lost our voices,' the women said. 'This year, we have been forbidden to eat redcurrants and strawberries. We are allowed to eat apples, but we have to wash them under running water, the same with tomatoes and cucumbers.'

I also learnt that in the village there was a farm with eighty-six cows, and a fattening centre for livestock with a hundred and thirteen head of cattle. The kolkhoz had been 113 per cent above its annual production target in the first half of the year. Where, before, ten to thirteen hundred kilos of grain per hectare had been harvested, that year it was eighteen hundred.

The more the women talked, the more convinced I became that a crime was being committed at that very moment. A crime against my fellow-countrymen. Was that the reason why I had been discouraged from coming here?

It turned out that the nursery school being built was very near to the villages of Bobyor and Vladimirovka, attached to the Kiev region and surrounded by barbed wire. The fields went right up to the barbed wire. Not far away was the village of Golubievichi. The women told me that new houses had been built there. But the people from the villages that had been evacuated had not moved into them. The houses stayed empty for a while, and eventually local people moved in. We were sixty kilometres from Chernobyl, only thirty kilometres from the thirty square kilometre forbidden zone.

Today, the village of Rudnia-Ososhnya no longer exists. The government has taken the decision to carry out an emergency evacuation. Emergency, after so many years of lies. Criminal lies.

I decided then, whatever the price, to publish the truth. Only true *glasnost* [openness] could save these people. Although this had been proclaimed in 1985 when Gorbachev took power, there was hardly a sign of it in this area in 1987.

For a whole month after my trip to Rudnia-Ososhnya, my husband and I spent every weekend in the villages of Narodichi district. We had painful meetings with people who were doomed, overwhelmed, betrayed. More than five years have passed since then, but I have forgotten none of the people I met, none of their stories. I have kept the notebooks I filled at that time, and they sweat blood, like the memories of people who have reached a great age and who no longer expect anything from life.

THREE

Desolation in the forest

THE autumn earth is covered with leaves of blood and gold. Its beauty is indescribable. To the left are fields, and further off, pastures and cattle grazing. Mist hangs over the forests which stretch away as far as the eye can see. A real picture. No, it's not Provence—far better, it's our forest region! Wide open spaces and forests, which arouse heart-rending feelings of filial affection. Set like a precious stone in this emerald landscape is the village of Khristinovka. Does its name come from 'Christian' or 'Christ'? From the word *khrest*, which means 'cross' in Ukrainian? What a cross this village has been condemned by fate to bear! To its right, in the distance, traditional wooden cottages and solid, white, kiln-fired brick houses peep from among the cherry and apple trees. This is the village of Staroye Sharnye. And straight ahead …

Straight ahead: 'Stop! No entry! Danger of death!' proclaims a noticeboard nailed to a barbed-wire gate locked with an enormous padlock.

No. It's not possible. It doesn't look real. There is a house, right nearby, on the other side of the barbed wire, just a hundred metres away. An apple has fallen into the garden, near the fence, and has rolled into the grass. A little boy comes out of the house. He is about five or six years old. He runs joyfully into the middle of the cascading autumn flowers. He is so sweet, he looks like a flower himself. His little hand reaches out towards the apple, he brings it to his mouth… the juice runs over his lips, falls on to his shoes, the grass. The little boy laughs…

The houses on the edge of the meadow on the other side of the barbed wire belong to the village of Novoye Sharnye, which stretches along the banks of the river Uzh. Since the accident at the

Chernobyl power station, it no longer exists. It is dead. This is the
sad fate of three other villages in the vicinity, Dolgiy Less, Motyli,
and Omelniki. I read in the newspaper that in summer 1986 two
hundred and fifty one families had been evacuated—over five
hundred people. Where had they been moved to, and how did
they live? That was what interested me above all. How had these
people adapted psychologically to their new dwelling-places?

On that first Saturday when I visited Narodichi for the first time
after the Chernobyl explosion, I did not get a proper idea of the
full scale of the catastrophe, or of the lie, even in our own area. On
that day of rest there was no-one from the local Executive
Committee around. That was why I simply spoke to people in the
street, in shops, and in their houses. I was advised to go first to the
edge of the district, to the hamlet of Mirni. Fifty cottages had been
built there for the evacuees. No-one wanted to live there. Why?

That is what I talked about at Mirni with the people who had
fled from the village of Novoye Sharnye. This is what they told
me:

Adam Pastushenko, a war invalid, who since he was evacuated
has worked at the Narodichi district finance department, said:
'They didn't have to build the houses there. For two reasons: first,
it's hardly any better than those we had to leave. Second, for years
there was a pesticide depot there for crop spraying aeroplanes. You
can't breathe the air there.'

Now that the evacuees had heard that a journalist from the
regional capital had arrived, they all gathered in the shop to tell me
their woes, to ask for help for all kinds of problems. And literally
all of them asked the same question: who gave the order, who
decided to build here, right next to a dangerous radioactive zone,
houses for people who had already suffered so much at the gates
of Chernobyl? I did not know the answer then, I was looking for
it myself. Here, in particular.

The peasants asked me to walk with them along the two roads
of the new village. Many of the houses were empty. In four of the
new buildings, the floorboards had been torn up and pesticide-
impregnated earth had been thrown out of the windows. One of

my companions joked: 'We don't even have flies here, they're all dead.' A light breeze wafted the nauseating smell of ammonia towards us.

In some houses it was very cold. The heaters had blown up. 'The bosses say that old people don't know how to use the heating properly and that's why the heaters blew up,' people complained.

In Zhukov Street, I was told, all the earth had had to be removed from eight houses after the floorboards had been pulled up. One of the evacuees, Fedor Zayichuk, invited me into his house, and showed me into three rooms. The ceilings were black. It was damp and cold. People were constantly asking me: 'How can we live here, how?'

After I had toured the houses, we went back to the shop. I wanted to know how the evacuees were provided with 'clean' food. The manager of the shop, Ludmila Pastushenko, complained that she was sent disgusting bread, burnt, inedible. There was no mineral water. There was not always enough meat to go round. Those who worked could not buy it in the daytime, and after work there was hardly ever any left. There was no smoked fish. No chickens. From time to time, there were ducks. There was fruit juice. The 'ration' allocated from on high was roughly as follows: One kilo of buckwheat and millet, two tins of condensed milk per month for each evacuee.

But what worried people most was their health and that of their children. Adam Pastushenko, the war veteran, told me that seventeen microcuries of caesium had been found in his body. He had spent twenty-four days at Zhitomir hospital. He had been let out with nine microcuries.

Nina Mokhoyid said: 'I've got two little girls, Olya, who is twelve, and Lyuda, nine. Olya recently had to stay in the children's hospital in the capital. Lyuda is sick too. We were given tablets to take for two months. The children are suffering from swollen thyroid glands.'

Valentina Kavka, who works at the local cultural centre, told me: 'My two children, Bogdan, six, and Svetlana, fourteen, have been sent to Zhitomir and Kiev. Bogdan has hypertrophy of the liver and an enflamed colon.'

They all came back to the same question: do they really have to evacuate us from a radioactive zone to here, literally only a few kilometres away from our old homes at Novoye Sharnye, surrounded by barbed wire?

What could I say to them?

I left the village of Mirni with a heavy heart.

People accompanied me as far as the centre of Narodichi, showing me the quickest way through the cottage-gardens. The nauseating smell of ammonia mingled with that of smoke. Little fires burned here and there: children were lighting bonfires like in Rudnia-Ososhnya. And radioactive ash was covering the surrounding area here too.

On Sunday, we went to other villages where houses had been built for people who had been evacuated.

The village of Mezhilesk (which means 'in the heart of the forest' in Ukrainian) lived up to its name. A layer of earth had been removed around the school and seven dwellings, six dilapidated houses had been demolished, and radioactive earth had been removed from one house. And despite this, Mezhilesk was considered 'clean'. The 25 per cent salary supplement and 30 roubles a month 'coffin allowance' was not paid here, as it was in the other villages under special control. Even telephones had been installed. (Every cloud has a silver lining.) There was also a clinic, but it had been closed for six months.

The summer after the explosion, fifteen houses had been built for evacuated people. The day I arrived, four of them were still uninhabited, after a whole year. Here are a few testimonies:

Nadyezhda Osadchaya, an accountant for the village council: 'The houses were built in a hurry, without thinking that country people would be living there. The old people spent all winter warming themselves at the village council offices. They need a stove, and there isn't one in those houses. No oven either. If there was central heating, there would be no problem. But the old people don't know how to use individual heaters. They should have put in stoves...'

Antonina Adamovna Kondratyenko, born in 1912, and Olympia Mikhailovna Zhovnirchuk, born in 1905, who was also present, nodded. Tears were gently running from their faded eyes.

Those houses that were lived in were mostly occupied by retired evacuees. There were only two or three of working age.

When the evacuees had been moved in, they had been given two piglets per family, crates of cabbages, cucumbers and tinned tomatoes, three sacks of corn, and a dozen chickens.

'It was really hard to leave our homes, our villages. If you had heard the cries, the din, the tears! When the lorry drew up in front of the house, we had to load in all our belongings. Our houses were better back there, they were well heated, we had everything we needed, we only had to buy bread. Here we have to buy everything,' said the two old ladies.

'One of the old women had just lost her husband, she had just gone to bury him at Dolgiy Less next to the family tomb. It's lucky they let her go.'

The local authorities in Mezhilesk, in their haste to look after the evacuees, had bought three houses from the collective farm on top of the fifteen newly-built ones, at twenty thousand roubles each. But the radiation victims did not move into them either. Two young couples from the collective farm took two and the third stayed empty.

Anatoly Konotovskiy, secretary of the party branch at the Mayak collective farm: 'This year the houses have been refurbished. they won't be cold this winter. The ceilings have been insulated and the doors have been rubbed down. The council's executive committee granted some money to buy firewood from the Ovruch forestry development scheme. We weren't allowed to get it from Narodichi because the wood there is radioactive. But the evacuees go and get it from the abandoned villages, Omelniki, Motyli. Even though it's forbidden! The radioactivity level there is very high. Stoves have been installed in the houses for the old women, traditional stoves. They will be given enough wood, they'll be able to keep warm all winter.

'Our village isn't under special control, but the children are ill.

They have been examined, and many were placed under observation. They all have swollen thyroid glands. There have been school medical inspections.

'Nearby is the village of Osoka. It belongs to our collective farm too. The level of radioactivity there is even higher than at Golubievichi, but they're not paid any salary supplement. The village isn't under special control, but we are forbidden to drink our milk or eat our meat and poultry. There is a farm in the village. We deliver the milk to the State, and then it is sent to Ovruch to be treated. We are brought milk from Korosten district.' Four years later, it was found that there too the level of radioactivity was higher than normal.

Vladimir Rudnitskiy, chair of the village soviet: 'The farm at Osoka employs eleven people, and keeps three hundred and fifty head of cattle. The farms at Mezhilesk and Osoka were cleansed. By the school the level of radioactivity was six times the norm. Some of the earth was removed.

'Although the evacuees have tickets to get food, nothing special is brought in for them. If they complain loudly enough, there is a delivery. There have been two deliveries of condensed milk to Mezhilesk, and some tins have come too.

'The milkmaids at Ossoka refused to work.

'In the village of Golubievichi, where twenty houses had been built for evacuees, the cows had been taken away on 6 August 1986, because the milk was radioactive. The children were kept at school all day and given three meals made from "clean" food. Free of charge.'

Maria Konotovskaya, an accountant for Golubievichi village council: 'For two or three months, we got an extra 25 per cent on top of our salary and 30 roubles for food. Then, suddenly, it was cut. We were told that it had been a mistake: it wasn't us that were meant to get the money, but another village, Buda-Golubievichi. Recently the land tax has been stopped. We can't eat our own products, but we don't get the 30 roubles.

'People didn't want to move into those new houses. They can see how we live here. And anyway, those houses are cold. Granny

Yuzefa is always asking to go back to her village. She says she'll come back later. In spite of her age—she was born in 1914—she helps out a bit on the collective farm.

'We had prepared such a welcome for the evacuees, with bread and salt, and flowers. We had been told that they would come in July or August. A day had been fixed, and then the Narodichi district party secretary came to tell us that the evacuees were not coming. And we had got a table ready, we had made bouquets of flowers, all the schoolchildren had come, the whole village had come out to welcome them. And there was nobody ...

'The houses stayed empty until autumn, then we let the village people move in. We waited until then...'

The same thing happened in the village of Guto-Maryatine.

Nina Volokh, postmistress: 'Twelve of the fifteen houses are occupied by young couples from the village. Only three families came here. There were flowers, bread and salt. The first secretary of the district committee, Anatoly Melnik, came. We have an orchestra which gave a concert in the street for the evacuees.'

Victor Tereshchenko, tractor driver: 'We come from the district of Brovarski, in the Kiev region. It's not a radioactive region, but we have only been married a short time and we have a little girl, Mashenka, who is eleven months old, and we had nowhere to live. So we decided to come here, because we knew there were empty houses and they needed extra pairs of hands. Valentina, my wife, stays at home with Mashenka, and I got work at the Mayak collective farm as a tractor driver. The house is cold. When it rains, water runs into the bedroom and on to the landing. In winter, I get up at three o'clock in the morning to light the heater. It is so cold that you can see your breath. In a month and a half we burned three barrowloads of wood. We have bottled butane gas, but you have to wait a month and a half to get a bottle. In winter, the water freezes in the water heater. The nearest well is two kilometres away. And we ought to bathe the baby every day.'

The evacuees moved out of house no. 7 for the same reasons. Nikolai Kharchenko, a pensioner form the evacuated village of

An abandoned kitchen in Chernobyl, 1990. The washing up is still in the sink.

Omelniki, moved to Tichkov with his wife. There he bought a normal, well heated house.

I remember the testimony of one woman pensioner particularly well: Maria Stepanovna Kozirenko, a former inhabitant of Dolgiy Less. 'They took us straightaway to the hamlet of Rozokhovski. We had no other place to go to. Those who had relatives elsewhere went to them. But people like us went to the hamlet of Rozokhovski. We stayed there about a week. With me was my

35

son's little boy, who is two and a half years old. We spent the summer at my son's house, and in the autumn, on 15 September, we came here. We miss our village a lot. There are four families from Dolgiy Less here. We are nearly all retired. Not a lot of young people. We were told that we would just have to leave for a short while, perhaps a few weeks, a month at the very most. The bus came for us on 27 May, at seven o'clock in the morning, and by ten o'clock we were gone. In the morning we wanted to take the cows to the pasture, but the militia took them back in. We also wanted to kill a little pig ...

'It's cold here, we're a long way from home, off the beaten track ...'

Maria could not hold herself back any longer, she started to weep, she wiped her tears and hid her tired face on the corners of her white headscarf with black polka dots.

At all costs, I had to complete my information-gathering by meeting the leaders of Narodichi district in order to find out their side of the story, and also to ask them to let me have a chart of radioactivity levels in the district, and perhaps the region as a whole. I was beginning to understand that we knew *nothing*, absolutely *nothing*, of the real situation after the explosion, of its scale and its consequences. The media were overflowing with shameful lies.

I could only meet the authorities during office hours, that is, when I was meant to be at my own desk. As I have said, I had no official pass to enter the contaminated regions. After racking my brains to find a way to get there, even for just one day (Narodichi is at the northern end of the region, five hours by bus from Zhitomir), I decided to ask for unpaid leave 'for personal reasons', but was met with a blunt refusal. The editor of my column wanted to know exactly what my reasons were. After a little while, I put in another request, as time was passing and I could find no other solution. The editor-in-chief did not dare to refuse a second time, as that had never happened to anyone before.

With my authorisation in my pocket, I left immediately for Narodichi, and once there I went to the district executive committee. It was 1 October 1987. I had promised to be on duty one Saturday to make up for my day off.

Valentin Semyonovich Budko, the chair of the executive committee of Narodichi district, proved to be a simple, sociable man who was truly distressed by what was happening in his area. Normally, the leaders of soviets or party secretaries just obey orders from higher up. No doubt Budko had also been this kind of functionary before the Chernobyl nuclear plant blew up. But the catastrophe, which had affected him personally, as well as his family and friends, this injustice, the silence surrounding the realities around him, had made a new man of him. He no longer thought just of his chairman's seat, but of his constituents.

I told him of my expedition to the living and dead villages of the district and I asked him about the health of the inhabitants and the levels of radioactivity. I told him that I would like to help the inhabitants by spreading light on this monstrous secret. Valentin Budko agreed to help me, at the same time remarking that other journalists had already visited, and that they had all collected information and had left promising to publish articles in their newspapers. But a year and a half later, nothing had been published anywhere. The only information about the children of the district had been given on 21 April 1987 in the paper *Kiev Evening*. It consisted of a declaration by the head of the department of mother and baby care at the Ukrainian Ministry of Health, G. Razumeyev, which ran as follows: 'The children of Pripyat and Chernobyl have not suffered. On the other hand, radioactive iodine has been found in the thyroid glands of some young inhabitants of the district of Narodichi. They were hospitalised immediately and are now out of danger.' That was all.

In the chairman's four-wheel-drive, we went to the evacuated village of Novoye Sharnye. On the way—it was eight kilometres—Valentin Budkov told me about that terrible day:

'I learnt about the accident at Chernobyl on the morning of 27 April. No, not from an official announcement. I was organising a fair for that day together with the first secretary of the party. So that was where we were in the morning. And suddenly, we saw a line of cars coming from the direction of Polyesye, in the Kiev region. Black "Volgas". One of the "Volgas" stopped, and Kolbasenko, the regional road transport chief, got out and told us that there had been a serious accident at the Chernobyl power station.

'But nobody told us what sort of accident, nor if it was dangerous. So the fair went ahead that day in Narodichi, with great success. All the villages of the district had brought produce: bacon, meat, cucumbers, tomatoes, cabbages, milk, cream cheese, butter, all kinds of vegetables, mushrooms, in short, everything that the forest region could offer at the height of socialism; and, at that moment, from what we were told by the district chief of civil defence, I. Makarenko, on 27 April 1986 at 4 pm, the level of radioactivity in Narodichi was three roentgens an hour. On the following day, 28 April at 9 am, the level was 0.6 roentgens. Everyone there was burnt by those pitiless rays, which destroyed all hope.'

When we arrived at the entrance to the village of Nozdrishchye, Valentin Budko pointed out something on the right:

'That's the most contaminated area in the whole district, 160 curies per square kilometre.'

I looked at the spot he was showing me. What I saw was a beautiful emerald green meadow stretching to the horizon. It had been drenched in caesium-137. On the meadow, mottled cows were browsing, carefree, lazily munching the radioactive grass. Two or three hundred metres further, behind barbed wire, was Novoye Sharnye. Our car stopped. Just before, the chairman had warned me: 'It might be better if you didn't get out.' I remember thinking, 'It's really weird, there are people living here, right by me, and I am told not to even get out of the car.' We got out.

By the heavily padlocked gate was a wooden sentry box with a notice saying 'No entry'. Through the window we could see telephones, a table, chairs. A policeman came out. I asked him for permission to cross the barbed wire. The gate opened, and we entered the zone. In the garden of the nearest cottage, radioactive fruit was falling uselessly into the overgrown grass. The branches were bent under the weight of what seemed like an exceptional harvest. Next to the boarded-up houses, the last chrysanthemums were blooming red-gold. They had gone back to their wild state and were almost as high as the windows. Here and there, we saw flower-beds full of wilted plants. In one courtyard a white cloth flapped in the wind. Big three-litre tins, washed by rain and snow, were fixed to the stakes of a fence. 'All the cats and dogs were put down two days after the evacuation,' the chairman told me.

This village is a monument. A monument to Chernobyl. A monument to a crime. The peasants who lived in this village had to pay for it dearly, too dearly.

Not far away, on the other side of the barbed wire, was the village of Nozdrishchye. Right by it was a newly-built nursery school. It was shown proudly to visitors, built as it was just two steps away from the radioactive meadow.

On the way back to Narodichi, the chairman told me how the villagers had been persuaded to leave:

'I myself handled the evacuation of four villages. I will tell you frankly that everything I saw and heard upset me. I remember an old woman who asked her neighbours to shut her up in her house. She didn't want to leave at any price, but we couldn't leave her in that hell. We got her out and took her with us.

'The first village that we evacuated was Dolgiy Less. It was a clear, sunny day. We arrived at six o'clock in the morning, before the villagers had had a chance to take their livestock out to the fields... The 27th was the turn of Novoye Sharnye. Everything was done in a hurry, we thought that the people would be coming back in a few weeks, and that was what we told them. We went from house to house reassuring them, but they were still nervous. The women were wailing like at a funeral, as if they were leaving for ever.'

It was indeed for ever. You have to have known such a trauma yourself to understand it. Their grandparents and great-grandparents had lived there, their ancestors had lived on the banks of those pure, beautiful Ukrainian rivers for thousands of years: the Uzh, the Zherev, the Noryn, the Rudenka. Every house was a work of art, with carvings decorating the outside, hand-woven rugs and embroidered serviettes indoors. For millennia people from this village had ploughed, sowed, harvested. There was practically no industry, the air was pure and clear. The forests had kept their original beauty and were bursting with mushrooms, wild fruit, and game. And all this had been wiped out in such a brutal, irresponsible, and definitive way. Will we ever be able to come to terms with that?

When we were back in his office, the chairman got out his map of the radioactive pollution over the whole district. It was almost completely covered with blood-red shading. There were only a few patches of green here and there, at the edges. I quickly jotted down the radioactivity levels in my notebook. At the edge of the map it read: 'maximum permissible norm of accumulated natural equivalent: 40 curies per square kilometre, lower limit, 15 curies per square kilometre.' We later learnt that in some areas the levels had reached 200 curies or even more. I saw that houses had been built for the evacuees in eight other nearby villages, of which half were listed as to be placed under strict control. Even the principal town of the district, near which a new hamlet, Mirni, had been built, and the village of Malye Kleshchi, had been put on the black list after the accident. And *just afterwards, in full knowledge*, cottages, baths, roads, nurseries, and water pipes had been built next to these devastated nests. These people were being sent from Charybdis to Scylla, from the frying pan into the fire.

At the time of my investigation, millions of roubles had already been invested in the building work in this dangerous zone, and there was no sign of it coming to an end. The building sites were advancing quickly, the workers were under pressure to speed up work. Every Thursday, the vice-chair of the executive committee for Zhitomir region, Giorgi Gotovchits, chaired a work-in-progress meeting at Narodichi. It was there, behind closed doors, that the fate of the unhappy ignorants was in effect decided. But why did they have to build there, of all places? Had it been impossible to find anywhere 'clean' in the region, in the entire republic, for these people who had already received one dose of radiation, and who had suffered for nearly a month at the doors of Chernobyl? It is difficult, even impossible, to find a rational explanation.

What I heard at the hospital and at the Narodichi child health clinic overwhelmed me even further. Here is the testimony of the doctors: it's October 1987.

Lyubov Golenko, head of the department of paediatrics at Narodichi district hospital: 'It is certain that we sustained a dose of radioactive iodine. In my opinion, thyroid problems have risen by around 60 per cent. The worst cases have been transferred to Kiev. I can't say if the zone is totally without danger for children. Outside specialists say that we will be able to tell in two to five years.'

Leonid Ishchenko, chief medical officer at Narodichi district hospital: 'We have examined all the children in the district several times. Eighty per cent are suffering from an enlarged thyroid. Before, this occurred in about 10-15 per cent of cases. In our opinion, it can only be due to the accident.'

Alexander Sachko, director of Narodichi district clinic: 'No-one is going to make me believe that our children are in perfect health, and that the increased cases of enlarged thyroid glands have no connection with the accident. You can't say that all is well. Not long ago, I looked at all the examinations of children for a week. In 180 cases out of 500, there was a change in the blood formula.'

'Do they know this in Zhitomir or in Kiev, at the Ukrainian Ministry of Health?' I asked.

'Of course,' the doctors replied. 'We see a lot of specialists, they take blood samples for analysis, but they don't always send the results afterwards. We are told that we are all suffering from radiophobia, that our children are well, and there is no need to worry.' I was shown the results of tests on children and adults to screen for caesium-137. Two sides of notes which burn your hands and your conscience. All five thousand children in the area had been exposed to radiation from iodine-131. One hundred and fifteen children had been put on a 'confidential' list, with an increased risk of thyroid problems: tumours, goitre, hyper- or hypothyroid which could lead to retarded development or other serious consequences.

I returned to Zhitomir with this overwhelming information. The next day, I went to the regional health department to try and find some answers. For some time I was passed from one specialist to another. No-one could, or no-one wanted to, give me any clear information. I think they were all afraid. I was fully convinced that all information concerning the situation in the affected areas had long since been classified as 'secret', and that this secret was well kept. When I was able to speak to the head of the department of maternal and child health, Victor Shatilo, his words only convinced me further: 'We have found no ailments linked to radiation. When we compare the figures for the four previous years, we find no rise. Hypertrophy of the liver can be explained by secondary factors... We have not noted any thyroid problems. The people responsible are all agreed that there can be no problem.'

And there we have it. It has not been noted. We have not found. There can be no. In short, nothing threatens our children's safety...

I wrote an article which included all I had seen and heard, but I was unable to get it published in my own paper. At the local party meeting, it was mentioned that I had been seen in some of the villages in Narodichi district. (As it happens, I was the only journalist on that party newspaper not to belong to the party.) Another correspondent, Vladimir Bazelchuk, was sent to the district in all haste, and wrote an article on the evacuees which toed the line, and which was published immediately. My colleague managed to reproach these unfortunates: the theme of his lengthy article, which took up half a page, was 'we have built them houses, and they dare to complain!'

After that, all I could do was to send my article to federal newspapers. One of them would have published it, but told me: 'It won't work, it's a forbidden topic.' It was now January 1988.

One fine day, I had a phone call from the Kiev correspondent of *Pravda*, Semyon Adinets, with whom I had the following conversation:

Deserted homes on a Chernobyl street, 1990.

'Vladimir Gubaryev has asked me to tell you that we can't publish your article.'

'Why not?'

'Because we're going to publish another one on the same topic.'

But in vain I studied *Pravda* every day—I found nothing which resembled it. Nobody would risk publishing an article calling for no new construction work in the contaminated areas, and to preserve the health of the evacuees. Whose responsibility is it? Vladimir Gubaryev, whom I had begged to publish my article that a hundred other papers had rejected, and save thousands of people from a radioactive hell, had not even paid me the courtesy of a written answer. Maybe it was more convenient to speak through a third person, without leaving any written trace?

43

Vladimir Gubaryev was not the only one. Not to be discouraged, I went to see the publishers of the magazine *Ogonyok*. I did not manage to see the editor-in-chief, Vitaly Korotich. I was sent to the features editor, Alexei Panchenko. He was an elderly, very nervous man. His telephone rang endlessly, and he only lifted the receiver to replace it immediately. He read my article and promised to publish it, but it was only one more lie. How many times did I ring him up and write to him from Zhitomir! In the end, I went back to Moscow. I had told myself that whatever the price, I would get to see the editor-in-chief, Vitaly Korotich, in person. After all, he was a Ukrainian like myself, from Kiev. Surely he must understand the importance of my mission.

I found him in a corridor, and we talked in the hallway. We talked about the Ukraine. The Kiev newspapers had started a campaign against him, and this interested him. But I didn't have any copies of these newspapers with me, and I was interested in something completely different: would my article on Narodichi be published, and when? Vitaly Korotich assured me: 'Yes, I know, Panchenko has the article, he's preparing it for publication.' Panchenko gave me his word again, and I went back to calling him from Zhitomir. I no longer even asked him to publish the article, but at least to send it back to me. The last time I went to the *Ogonyok* offices, Panchenko searched for a long time in all his drawers, but he could not find it. In the course of the conversation he told me that it was impossible to publish it, because 'Dolgikh was down there and he didn't see anything in the papers like what I described in my article.' He then told me that he knew our first secretary, Vasili Kavun, and had done an article about him when was working for *Pravda*. I understood then that my article 'had been lost' for good as far as *Ogonyok* was concerned.

I never got a reply to my last letter to the magazine's editors, but I didn't expect anything else. My article did not appear in *Ogonyok*, but it was my own paper which suddenly printed a report by my boss on the district of Narodichi, in almost exactly the same vein as before. That was a job well done!

After this, I decided to tackle the *Literaturnaya Gazeta*. But there too I obtained only promises. No-one wanted us and our Chernobyl. Nor our children.

During one of my stays in Moscow, despairing of my total powerlessness to change anything, I went to the main post office and sent one more registered letter, this time to the address of a famous poet, Yevtushenko. I got no reply. But during the 1990 elections, I went to the town where he was staying to give him my support (for me the elections were over, and I had a little time to breathe). After his victory, I asked him why he had not answered my letter. He assured me that he had never received it. 'If you sent it to Moscow, it might have got lost, because I am always at my dacha in Peredelkino. I only go to my Moscow flat to pick up the post...'

It is probable that my cry for help was lost between a Moscow flat and the outlying dachas. It is the Post Office which is to blame. The Ministry of Post and Telecommunications.

[The author eventually managed to have an article published in Pravda and another in Isvestia. They had wide repercussions and also had the effect of launching a whole campaign against her in Zhitomir. Attempts were made to make her resign her post at the newspaper. When she stood for election in March 1989, attempts were made to discredit her, but in vain; she was elected. Once in parliament, she used her platform to denounce the criminal negligence committed against the population of the regions neighbouring Chernobyl, and even sent President Gorbachev a videotape showing the consequences of the catastrophe in the district of Narodichi. The various commissions set up to study the measures to be taken were particularly ineffective, sweeping all information under the carpet. Experts battled it out to determine what constituted an 'acceptable' dose of radioactivity. At the second session of the Congress of People's Deputies, which met in spring 1990, Alla Yaroshinskaya, with other members of parliament, was successful in getting approval for the formation of a Commission responsible for dealing with the consequences of the catastrophe, chaired by herself. The battle continues, as new attempts are constantly being made at high level to play down the extent of the consequences of Chernobyl.]

FOUR

Crime without punishment

W HATEVER level of the hierarchy you approach, the logic is the same. This is the way the system has worked for years.

Yet I did not give up. I went to the Energy Resources Office of the Council of Ministers of the USSR and spoke to its vice-chair, V. Marine, a member of the government commission dealing with the consequences of the accident at the Chernobyl nuclear power station. He called in one of his heads of department and a colleague, Y. Dyokhtyarev.

Vladimir Marine declared that *it was only the local authorities who had decided in 1986 where to build the evacuees' houses*, and that the inhabitants of twelve villages were due to be evacuated between 1990 and 1993. They spared no efforts to try and convince me that it had never been forbidden to publish facts on the consequences of the tragedy. They declared earnestly that any peasant could obtain all the information they wanted from their village soviet. From the mouth of an official, this was a shameless lie, or else proof of total ignorance. When I mentioned the restrictions (formulated particularly by the government commission which Marine belonged to), he replied that they were no longer in force. It was strange to say the least that I, as a journalist, had been unable to have my article on Narodichi published in the Soviet Union for two years, if any collective farm worker could simply have any information he or she could wish for!

I left this interview with a feeling of unease. I understood that it would be a long time before the fragile shoots of *glasnost* put out by the Congress of People's Deputies were out of danger of suffocation. In fact, nobody was interested in the doctors' findings or the official documents I had presented to parliament.

On 10 August 1989, the members of the government commission for emergencies came to Narodichi to meet representatives of the five districts affected by the radioactivity. Despite everything, the pressure of the Byelorussian and Ukrainian deputies for openness, together with the first serious articles which were now appearing in the papers, had at last persuaded the government to remember its citizens living in the affected zones.

The meeting was arranged for 11 o'clock, but long in advance the hall in the House of Culture was full to overflowing. Crowds were gathering in the street, where loudspeakers had been set up. They were impatient to see the recently appointed head of the governmental commission, V. Doguzhyev. What would he say?

The commissioners were late, and the crowd began to get worried. Journalists from Zhitomir and Kiev were there, as well as Ukrainian national TV news cameramen. At last it was announced that the helicopters had landed. (A special landing pad had been set up the day before.)

On the stage, a long table had been covered with a red cloth, and behind it, a few chairs were awaiting the guests. But when the commissioners entered by the side door and started to take their places, it became clear that the organisers had made a mistake, the number of chairs was far too small. More were quickly brought and were set up in four rows, but some of the commissioners still had to sit in the main hall.

The number of people who had come should have demonstrated the growing concern of the government for the victims, but not all those present fully appreciated this, and accusations and reproaches verging on insults began to rain down. I cannot pass judgement on these people; for three years they had built houses, with public gas and all modern conveniences, in contaminated areas. In short, everything had been done to create an illusion of care and safety. They had been deceived right down the line.

I had not intended to speak, but I was asked to. The chair of the session was V. Yamchinskiy, then head of the executive committee of Zhitomir district soviet. At his side, in the centre, sat the first secretary of the regional committee of the party, Vasili Mikhailovich Kavun, a member of the central committees of the communist parties of the Soviet Union and of the Ukraine. When the chair introduced them, the room buzzed with indignation, and someone shouted: 'He's come at last, after three years!'

During my speech, I asked several questions of the first secretary: Why, for nearly a month after the catastrophe, had the children of Narodichi continued to breathe in radioactive dust, to eat contaminated food—why hadn't they been evacuated straight away? Why had the secretary, who was on holiday abroad, not returned immediately after the explosion to take away the children? No-one had wanted to assume responsibility for this in the boss's absence. I asked him also just who had taken the decision to build houses for the evacuees on radioactive land. Why did he, the first secretary, say that he had not seen the map of radioactivity in the district of Narodichi, when I, a simple reporter from a provincial newspaper, had seen it at the district executive committee?

The room was in uproar. This was no doubt the first time that Vasili Kavun had heard himself addressed in this way in public. He rose to his feet and started to explain in a low voice that *the decision to build had been taken with the agreement of the governmental commission...* And that there was no map of the radioactive zones. He had no information at his disposal, he was away at the time of the explosion and he 'had not been able to find transport to return home', he had come back after twelve days when construction was already under way...

Pull the other one, as they say. Hadn't the subordinates of the first secretary of the region been consulted, and hadn't he been shown the map of radioactive contamination? Or perhaps it was simpler to wash his hands of the whole affair? Who was it who was misleading us: the vice-chair of the Commission for Energy Resources of the Council of Ministers of the USSR, who had explained to me that it was the *local* authorities who had chosen the sites for the houses; or the first secretary of the party regional committee?

An article published by the newspaper *Trud* on 2 August 1989, entitled 'Villages under strict control', read:

Nevertheless, ever since the following spring, the Commission of the Council of Ministers of the USSR and the Executive Committees of the regions of Zhitomir and Kiev had been in possession of a detailed map of radioactive pollution in the northern parts of the Ukrainian Forest. The map showed the villages and fields where the level of caesium-137 was higher than the margin of 40 to 100 curies. It was already clear that it was impossible to live or work permanently in these areas. Particularly in the villages of Yasyen and Shevchenko (Polyesye district, Kiev region) and in Minki, Shishalovkye, Velikiye Kleshchi and Polyessko (Narodichi district, Zhitomir region). And yet, people still live there.... . In any case, even without a map, the regional leaders and civil defence headquarters knew that between 27 and 29 April 1986, in the courtyard of the district Executive Committee, the level of background gamma radiation was higher than one roentgen an hour—twenty times higher than the level at which emergency evacuation should take place.

They knew! Today, when I re-read the TASS report of the press conference held on 6 May 1986 at the press centre of the Ministry of Foreign Affairs, I never fail to be astonished at *the way it all happened*. 'Officials' announced that 'during the last 24 hours, the level of radioactivity has once more decreased.' The vice-chair of the Council of Ministers of the USSR, B. Shcherbina, issued a statement: 'A rise in the level of radioactivity has been recorded in the area adjacent to the accident site, where the maximum levels of radioactivity reached between ten and fifteen milliroentgens an hour. On 5 May [1986], the level of radioactivity in these regions decreased by a factor of two to three.' Subsequently, if we are to believe official reports, the level fell daily. One would even believe that it has completely disappeared, evaporated. But why—this question has never ceased to torment me—why, three years after the accident, was it suddenly decided to evacuate the inhabitants?

Is it possible that the 'officials' did not know that in the streets of Pripyat, throughout 26 April and each of the following days, the level of radioactivity was more than 0.5 to 1 roentgen an hour? (cf. G. Medvedev, 'Chernobyl notebook', in *Noviy Mir*, no. 6, p36.)

Back to the meeting on 10 August 1989 in Narodichi. The whole of the governmental commission, led by its chair V. Doguzhyev, was present. Yevgeniy Kachalovski, vice-chair of the Council of Ministers of the Ukraine, took the floor. His speech made everyone present feel ashamed for this high official who bore a large part of the responsibility for the sufferings of our children. I am sure that it is only in our country, where the patience of the people is inexhaustible, that such leaders can exist.

Kachalovski tried first of all to blame everything on foreigners (I am transcribing directly from a tape): 'I will tell you: it's not by chance that the foreigners are now spending their dollars to study our achievements in this domain, because...' He was unable to continue with such sacrilege. To come to the most contaminated region for the first time in three years and then not to find anything else to say! He should have apologised and announced concrete measures to allow these people to live. But this 'big boss' had understood nothing. The room was buzzing, and, doubtless in order not to compromise the other 'big bosses' in Moscow, he began to lecture the assembly: 'Behave yourselves. If you don't want me to speak, I'll be quiet, but there's no point in shouting, we're not in the marketplace. You have come to hear me speak. If you don't like what I'm saying, go away. Or I could go and sit down, and you can have your say. What's all this noise? There's the ringleader, the woman by the microphone: when she raises her arms, everyone shouts, and when she lowers them, everyone is quiet. Is this the way to behave?'

What a way to speak to people you have deceived—and with never a second thought! Kachalovski continued: 'Consequently, it's not a matter of asking if the decision we took at that moment was a good or bad one, or whether we evacuated enough people. All the more so because it was the governmental commission, the central committee of the Communist Party of the Soviet Union, which took the decision, and it was also they who in the end decided the number of villages and people to evacuate; we only made proposals, which were then revised downwards.'

He then read from a piece of paper which had been passed to him: 'Our children have suffered more from this accident than any of the children from this zone. They started to be evacuated on 24 May, and the evacuation continued until 9 July 1986. At the height of the danger, the children were in the zone, and no-one warned us of the danger.'

No intelligible answer.

Yet it was Yevgeniy Kachalovski himself who was running the governmental commission responsible for dealing with the effects of the Chernobyl explosion in the Ukraine. But it was only the arrival on 2 May 1986 of the members of the Politburo, the chairman of the Council of Ministers, Nikolai Rizhkov, and the secretary of the Central Committee, E. Ligachev, which forced the leaders of the republic to visit the area.

Kachalovski was asked another question, similar to the previous one: 'Why were our children evacuated later than the children from Kiev region and Byelorussia, who left in the first half of May 1986? Who personally took the decision for our district?'

For an answer, we were treated to a verbal frenzy: 'I will tell you that we were presiding over the May Day ceremonies. The whole Politburo was there. Our wives, our children, our grand-children, and the same question is being asked in Kiev: who gave the order to hold the parade, because it was not called off, and nobody, not our scientists, or our specialists, those comrades who are now making such fine speeches, three years later [sic.] They are like firefighters who arrive when the house has already burnt down, comrades, and here, where you live... they are very clever, but yesterday, when they came before the fire, they did not know. It's easy to be wise after the event. You understand, you too could have protested then... Neither did we know what was going to happen, where the radioactivity was, in what amounts, you neither, you didn't make any proposals, even after the parade. You didn't even come six months later, but only after three years, and that's why the parade took place.'

I listened, dying of shame, to this incoherent reply from Katchalovski, and couldn't help thinking of the events of a month earlier. On 12 June 1989, the first session of the Supreme Soviet of the USSR was investigating the candidature of Yuri Izrael for the post of chair of the State Committee for Hydrology and Meteorology. The deputies from the Ukraine and Byelorussia asked the same questions about Chernobyl: why did nobody know of the existence of the maps showing radioactive contamination? Why had no information on levels of radioactivity been made public? Who had taken the decision to carry on with the May Day parade? Why had the children of Kiev not been evacuated earlier? And so on.

FIVE

'No threat to health'

DURING the second session of the Congress of People's Deputies in spring 1990, a truly theatrical performance took place within the walls of our Soviet Parliament. The main actors were: Yuri Antonievich Izrael, the chair of the state Committee for Hydrology and Meteorology, who was canvassing for a second term of office, and Valentina Shevchenko, a member of the Ukraine Politburo, and Nikolai Rizhkov, Chair of the Council of Ministers of the USSR and a member of the Politburo of the Soviet Union.

The outbursts of allegations which hurtled to and fro before the shocked eyes of the deputies (what is more, the entire session was being transmitted by television to the whole Soviet Union) was very revealing. When Izrael, who had been pushed into a corner by Valentina Shevchenko, was forced to say to whom he had passed the information on the day after the catastrophe, she started to accuse him in an impassioned voice of having signed a report in the presence of the Academy member Iline, which claimed that the situation in Kiev and the surrounding region presented no danger to the health of the population, including the children.

'Surely you remember,' she said. 'I was sitting opposite you and I asked you: "Yuri Antonievich, what would you do if your grandchildren were in Kiev?" You didn't reply. The political leaders in the Ukraine carried out all the other decisions taken by the governmental commission to the letter, working day and night, and with the backing of the political leadership of the country.' Sensing that punishment was near, they let loose a flood of mutual denunciations in front of parliament.

In fact, Valentina Semyonovna Shevchenko represents a rural

area in the Kiev region, and Chernobyl is in her constituency. This is what her constituents wrote in a collective letter addressed to the Supreme Soviet: 'We have a deputy in the Supreme Soviet of the USSR, Valentina Shevchenko, but she has never been to see us. Neither were we able to meet her in Moscow. We informed her of the date and time of our visit and we waited for her for a whole day at 27, Kalinin Avenue [where the committees of the Supreme Soviet of the USSR meet], but we later learnt that she had left that day for Kiev. We can no longer rely on her help.'

At the end of her impassioned speech, in which you would have searched in vain for a word of regret, Valentina Shevchenko declared: 'I think that today, Yuri Antonievich, who occupies such a high government post, and who is responsible for an exceptionally important sector, should no longer be satisfied with a compromise, but adopt a principled stand. And I shall vote against you, Yuri Antonievich!' This remark was greeted with applause. The applause was for a woman who bore a large part of the responsibility for the poor state of health of numerous children, who for years had hidden the real situation in the contaminated zones!

After Valentina Shevchenko, Nikolai Rizhkov, chair of the Council of Ministers of the Soviet Union, spoke. He parried the attack energetically: 'We are speaking here of events on May 7. I do not know what happened at the meeting of the Ukrainian Politburo, as I wasn't there. But I do know that I was with you on 2 May. Do you remember? Do you recall that I came to see you with the political leadership? Therefore, it was before 7 May.' Finally, he expressed the firm conviction that 'he [Izrael] could not be held responsible for Chernobyl.'

Like many deputies, no doubt, I immediately asked myself: 'Who then?' Who is guilty of the lack of information, who made the whole country overflow with counter-truths, who gave the order to keep the secret? Who, in the end, will take the blame? The situation is as follows: there are people who are ill, there people who have been deceived, and there are no culprits. Only the underlings are being blamed. And not only in the case of Chernobyl.

The debates on Izrael's nomination continued. One deputy, exposing the qualities of the candidate, declared: 'What I am going to say will probably come as a revelation to you. It concerns the situation of the whales, saving the whales on the coast of Alaska. Three hours after the telephone call from the American section of Greenpeace, our ice-breakers were called off course on Izrael's order, in order to go and save the whales. After three hours. The government decision was only taken three days later. Perhaps I am revealing a secret. Perhaps chairman Rizhkov doesn't even know about it. It was a risky action, but it paid off. The repercussions throughout the world were immense, comrades.'

The deed is evidently to the credit of its author, or at least it would have been if the shameful chapter of Chernobyl had not previously appeared in Izrael's life. It is indeed noble to save whales, but perhaps he should also have worried about the thousands of children and adults who have lost their health?

Yuri Antonievich Izrael was re-elected. Four hundred and twenty-two deputies took part in the vote. 294 voted for, and 86 against. There were 42 abstentions.

Before announcing a break, the vice-chair of the Supreme Soviet of the USSR, A. Lukyanov, gave three minutes to the deputy for the Autonomous Republic of Checheno-Ingushetiy, S. Khadzhev, who was director-general of the Grozneftekhim chemical plant in the Northern Caucasus, in order to explain his vote. His brief contribution constitutes an epilogue to the drama:

'We have just elected Yuri Antonievich, and by doing so, we have approved all that has been done to our people, our lands, our rivers, our lakes, and our seas. We have ratified all that. It was he who confirmed what was happening, he was in the know, and we weren't. For example, I only learnt what had happened in 1988. But he knew everything, and he only felt obliged to report to his superiors. That was the limit of his responsibility, and now we have given our approval... I don't know how you will be able to look your constituents in the eye... That's why I consider that today, we have forgotten our electorate, we have forgotten the millions of sick children, our brothers and sisters now in hospital.

We have forgotten them. We should have appreciated the competence of Yuri Antonievich, but have said to him: "Comrade Yuri Antonievich! You don't have a sense of civic responsibility, your heart is not affected by the plight of your fellow citizens. This is how it has been for fourteen years: you have kept silent, and you have contented yourself with reporting to your superiors." '

But nothing could alter the decision taken one minute earlier by the deputies of the Supreme Soviet.

SIX

The moment of truth?

I F Elena the Beautiful, heroine of the Russian stories, had had a grandmother, she would certainly have been Elena the Wise. This is what the deputies privately call Elena Borisovna Burlakova, professor of biology. In this chapter I would like to give you some idea of the character of this amazing woman.

I first heard of her a few years ago, at the Narodichi district council offices, when I was being shown a letter addressed to the group for defending the population against radioactivity. In the years following the Chernobyl catastrophe, dozens of organisations and local authorities had appealed for help from all kinds of sources, but nobody had paid them the courtesy of a reply. And now, without an appeal for help at all, a letter had come for this group from a professor, the chair of the Scientific Council for Radiological Problems of the Academy of Sciences of the USSR. It was dated July 1989.

Elena Burlakova told us in her letter that after a visit by some scientists, the Council she chaired had sent a letter to parliament and a few other places, 'asking them to resolve the question of the evacuation of people living in the contaminated areas as soon as possible'. 'Furthermore,' the professor wrote, 'we are in the process of organising a trip to your region, as well as installing a group of geneticists and ophthalmologists there, to try and determine the real doses of radioactivity that the inhabitants have been subjected to. This question is not easy to answer, and we are in discussion with the institutes of the Academy of Sciences and the Centre for Eye Microsurgery.'

I remember that this letter astounded me. Dozens of scientists had come and gone, but there had never been any follow-up, and even if they did take a few analyses they did not usually send the results. Elena Burlakova's letter was the first letter we had had from a scientist which bore the stamp of human feelings, compassion, and a desire to help.

From summer 1989 onwards, Professor Burlakova, assisted by the scientific secretary of the Council for Radiological Problems, V. Nayidich, had written to six addressees: the Committee of the Supreme Soviet for Ecology and Rational Utilisation of Natural Resources; the President of the Academy of Sciences of the USSR, G. Marchuk; the Ecology Commission already mentioned; the deputies Boris Yeltsin and Vasili Belov [a famous writer on country matters]. This letter announced that the Council for Radiological Problems had discussed the results of its visit to the district of Narodichi in Zhitomir region. The scientists had decided that 'it is imperative to evacuate the inhabitants of Narodichi district to uncontaminated areas.' It is not difficult to imagine the nervous reaction that this letter provoked in high circles. And yet, after a while, the decision was taken to evacuate twenty-four villages and the principal town of the district, and to settle the people in an uncontaminated region. To cut a long story short, I can confirm that this evacuation has already started.

But Elena Burlakova and a few of her colleagues who had visited Narodichi had written this particular letter, full of sorrow, to the corresponding member of the Academy of Sciences of the USSR, A. Yablokov, vice-chair of the Committee of the Supreme Soviet for Ecology and Rational Utilisation of Natural Resources. I would like to quote him too, to show what a scientific eye outside the circle of 'official' medicine is able to register.

Let us start with the emotional aspect. The most terrible effects are not mutant animals—blind piglets, a foal with eight legs, calves without tails and with hare lips, cats and dogs with all sorts of monstrosities—the most terrible thing is the cry of a young woman: 'I want to live, I'm still young!' And the cry which pierces your heart: 'Our children are dying! Help!' Even more terrible are the tears of a doctor describing five categories of children whose thyroids have received doses of fifty to a hundred roentgens of radioactive iodine, or those with peritonitis.

Before my eyes a young woman is wailing, full of despair: 'I am a farmer, give me work, I want to touch the earth! My children are dying!' It is terrible to see grown men cry. These lands resound with the sound of crying and wailing. The population is united in the claim: 'We demand the right to live. We demand to be evacuated!'

The leaders of the Ukrainian Ministry of Health, the 'official' medical experts, and the representatives of the Department of Agriculture and Food, have lost the confidence of the population. They are treated like scoundrels, criminals, they are accused of knowingly under-estimating the doses of radioactivity. All the more so since the majority of medical measures taken with regard to the people living in the zones under strict control only exist on paper (in particular iodine treatment).

We consider it our duty to draw your attention to the following facts:

1. The gradual rise in cases of deformities in new-born animals.
2. The increase in eye problems among the population, in particular among children; and an equivalent rise in cases of pneumonia, pharyngitis, nosebleeds, dizzy spells, bouts of tiredness, and so on. In the adult population, tumours of the larynx among people working on sheep farms.
3. The decision to keep the population inside these zones relies on prognoses of the evolution of the radioactive pollution, without taking into account the first shockwave of radioactivity. The deposits of radioactive strontium, plutonium, and caesium were not taken into account at all, which led to a perceptible underestimate when calculating the doses of radiation received.
4. The population receives practically no 'clean' food: two

tins of corned beef per person per month, plus one orange per child, it's simply an insult. People are forced to give their children locally produced milk, and to eat contaminated food.

5. In order to establish a scientific prognosis of the radiobiological consequences, it is absolutely necessary to be in possession of concrete information on the levels of ionising radiation in the contaminated zones of Ukraine, Byelorussia, and Russia. Even those data which are currently available cannot be consulted by the radiobiologists from the Academy of Sciences, nor by the majority of scientists from the Ministry of Health and the Academy of Medicine.

6. It is criminal to forbid the publication of statistical data relating to infant and adult sickness rates, particularly eye complaints.

7. It is a matter of urgency to carry out an analysis of radioactivity levels in the contaminated territories, taking into account the total number of radionuclides.

8. It is imperative, when calculating the maximum acceptable dose, to take into account the first wave of radioactivity, which the doctors do not, and equally all the possible contributory effects which might make the contamination worse: stress, pesticides, nitrates, vitamin deficiency, bad hygiene (two pieces of soap per person per month, etc.).

9. Measures must be taken urgently to evacuate the population to 'clean' areas, and to create reserves in the contaminated areas where scientists from all disciplines can carry out research into the consequences of the accident. Foreign scientists could also be involved in this. [...]

The future of our children who live some distance away from the regions affected by the Chernobyl catastrophe is also at stake.

This was the position adopted by the scientists.

Elena Burlakova's first trips to the contaminated zones had a great effect. She touched the weary hearts of the children of Chernobyl, and Iline [who took the official line] found her a formidable opponent. Formidable for two reasons: as a scientist of high standing, and as an independent person out of reach of orders from on high.

It was the party committee of Narodichi district that passed me a copy of Professor Burlakova's letter. At that time, the popular science journal *Therapeutic Archives* had already published, in volume 59, no. 6 (1987), an article by some of Professor Burlakova's colleagues, M. Brillant, A. Vorobyev and E. Gogine, entitled 'Long-term consequences of low-level ionising radiation on man'. And V. Shevchenko, a doctor of biology and head of the laboratory of genetic biology at the Institute of General Genetics at the Academy of Sciences of the USSR, had prepared an article for the review *Priroda* (Nature) based on his observations in Narodichi district on the influence of low-level radiation on animals. Other scientists were also working on this topic. In short, without any preconceived ideas, all those who had visited the contaminated zones were concentrating on the children who by now had languished there for several years.

It was thus that the debate began between those who supported a limit of 35 rems, and those who understood that this was unacceptable and were desperately looking for solutions without constantly thinking of the costs of evacuation to the public purse, who cared about the health of the people and were asking why it had deteriorated to such an extent and if there was a direct or indirect link with radioactivity levels.

Elena Burlakova and her colleagues went to the contaminated zones several times, wrote to numerous civil servants, and demanded access to secret results of tests carried out on these unwilling guinea-pigs.

I first saw Elena Burlakova at the State Planning Committee, at a session of the commission of experts on which we all sat. She had a typically Russian face, frank and open, grey hair tied back in a bun, and a severe black dress. Each time she spoke, she sounded

*This slogan on the wall of the Chernobyl nuclear plant reads:
'Communism will triumph!'*

emotive, as if it was for the first time. Sometimes very emotive. To
such an extent that I also began to feel worried when I listened to
her. Honesty was her foremost quality.

It was largely due to Elena Burlakova's findings that the commission concluded that the concept of '35 rems in 70 years' was
profoundly flawed. She and her colleagues, among whom were a
large number of scientists from Byelorussia and the Ukraine, tried
for many years to prove that the estimate of risk from radiation, and
the long-term consequences of the Chernobyl accident, depended
on a large number of factors. Their conclusions were included in
the commission's report. But afterwards? If we rejected the
proposals of 'official' medicine, we had to provide another solution,
and quickly. The people living in the zone could not wait.

The report of the commission of experts included recommendations on decisions to be taken as a matter of urgency in the next

two years. These were based on a composite theory about the effects of low doses of radiation sustained daily for a number of years.

On 1 September 1990, a decree was adopted by the Praesidium of the Supreme Soviet of the USSR: 'The creation of a commission to examine the causes of the Chernobyl accident and to judge the acts of officials responsible during the period following it.' Some scientists were appointed to this commission, among them Elena Burlakova and her colleagues, which was only logical.

On 23 January 1991 the regular session of the parliamentary commission took place. Professor Burlakova presented an important report on the effects of low-level radiation on the human body. Her report was based on a wide range of data which she had collected over the past two years, and in particular on examinations of people living in the most contaminated areas, including the 'liquidators'. What we heard was like a glimmer of truth, the first since the catastrophe. Her findings awakened unprecedented scientific interest, both in the Soviet Union and worldwide, and I shall go into them in some detail and in the professor's own words. Some readers may find this tedious, but, as I have said, it is extremely important.

The following questions were put to scientists: Was the evacuation carried out quickly enough? Had measures been taken to reduce the doses of iodine, particularly for children? What had been the effect of the 35 rem theory on the health of the population? 'I want to say straightaway,' declared Elena Burlakova, 'that according to our survey of doctors in the Ukraine, the Russian Federation, and in Byelorussia, the preventative iodine treatment was either not carried out at all, or in a very limited fashion. What is more, in the regions of the Russian Federation where treatment did begin, it was interrupted on the orders of the hierarchy, as the doctors bluntly told us, "in order to avoid panicking the population". Given the lack of training sessions to explain how to use iodine as preventative medicine, many cases of burnt mucous membranes occurred. Some areas only started treatment three or four months after the accident. All this is of course the responsibility of "official medicine".'

The scientists also had to answer a second question. Had they previously had experience of similar phenomena, whose observation could have helped doctors deal with the Chernobyl accident and its consequences with more confidence, and to help them find solutions? This shows that the novel nature of the situation had given rise to many doubts and questions as to the correct course to follow; apart from that, the data used were frequently incorrect.

As Elena Burlakova explained: 'In order to find out if anything was known on the topic, we studied in great detail the state of health of the population of the Techa region, which sustained radiation poisoning [from 1949 to 1951] as a result of radionuclide waste being dumped in the river, and that of the zone contaminated after the Kyshtim accident [1957], as well as the residents of the "Eastern Urals radioactive sector". By analysing the data, we discovered a large number of interesting facts which no-one had paid attention to at the time.'

It was found that a chronic irradiation syndrome had been diagnosed in people who had lived on the banks of the River Techa six to eight years before the dumping of the radionuclides. The development of the symptoms was clear to see. Many seemed later to have disappeared, but the diagnosis was clear: these were the first symptoms of a chronic ailment, even if they were confused and unknown to medical literature.

In all the publications on this subject, it was stated that chronic irradiation syndrome appeared at a threshold of a radiation level of one hundred roentgens. However, when the people living by the River Techa were examined, the syndrome was diagnosed in people who had received widely differing doses, often well below this threshold level.

Professor Burlakova continued: 'This made us think that it was impossible to speak of a universal threshold level. There were grounds to suppose that in the case of the people living by the River Techa, those suffering from certain ailments, or those with predispositions to these ailments, could, in a given ecological situation, develop the chronic irradiation syndrome when exposed to much lower levels of radiation. The study of the situation in the

Urals had thrown up a second important circumstance: the appearance or worsening of several cases of illness which are not described in Soviet radio-biological literature, nor itemised as linked to radiation exposure.

'What conclusions do the doctors draw? It is possible that the radiation factor plays a role in the development of pre-existing conditions. However, in other cases, where these conditions are less frequent, this phenomenon may be absent. This is the second fact denied by "official medicine". Thirdly, the seriousness of the condition is not directly dependent upon the radiation dose sustained, and this was not taken into account either.'

By comparing the medical cases observed after the radioactive waste spillage into the Techa with the Chernobyl explosion, Professor Burlakova had come to the conclusion that a similar range of ailments was about to appear. In the Ukraine, the number of cardiovascular complaints had risen by 80 per cent, and problems with the endocrine glands had doubled, especially diabetes. There was a whole spectrum of medical problems where the number of cases was perceptibly higher. For example, nobody had ever proved that heart attacks can follow exposure to radiation. Yet analysis of the data from the Techa region gives every reason to think so. A significant rise in infectious diseases was also recorded in the Techa region, and the same was confirmed at Kiev and in other places. Why, then, does 'official medicine' draw no conclusions in these cases?

She went on: 'The data obtained from the study of neurological syndromes are very interesting. There was a sharp increase in cases by the Techa, where the radiation level was only seven roentgens. We were assured that this is quite simply a reaction by the body's defence mechanism. Why then, when the same results were obtained at Chernobyl, were we assured then that it was only alarmist articles in the press which were panicking the population?

'It is very important to note that the official line maintained that there is a linear relationship between dose and effect: with higher levels of radioactivity, the effects are more serious. This enabled them to say that in areas where the level of radioactivity was low, any medical problems were not due to radiation, but to other factors.

'When we analysed the data from the Techa region, the area surrounding Chernobyl, and the region of Bryansk, we could see that the range of medical problems induced by the radiation is approximately the same, even if Soviet science does not link them with radiation. If there is no link, then we have to ask what can have caused them. This question can be approached from several points of view. Firstly, we can suppose that our medical statistics are so inadequate that certain theories cannot be confirmed: thus, each time a rise in a particular malady is discerned, the figures are declared unreliable, and that consequently they cannot be used to prove the influence of radioactivity. It can also be assumed that the officially declared doses are not correct. We are currently in possession of comparative data on genetic changes in the lymphocytes and in the teeth; these are linear data. But the changes do not coincide with the stated levels of radiation. They sometimes correspond with doses ten times higher. This is what worried Professor Vorobyev when she examined the children: from the information available to her, she assumed that they had been exposed to levels of radiation far higher that those stated. In fact, the level of the initial dose from the accident is still unknown. [As of April 1993, the doses of external radiation and internal contamination sustained by the residents in the first months after the disaster are still unknown.]

'Why should there be such a mismatch in the data? If we do not ask this question, we are deceiving the population, making them believe that all their ills are due to fear. Is our population the most nervous in the world? On the contrary, I would say that they are distinguished by their total scorn of danger, as they are even prepared to go onto contaminated land if they can pick good fruit there. Why, then, do we find this increased incidence of a variety of illnesses in the contaminated areas? Why can't we explain the situation from the radiological data, from international statistics on degrees of risk established by international commissions?

'I will now go on from factual data to experimental research. A whole series of experiments on animals have shown that with very low levels of radiation, ten to a hundred times higher than normal, there is no simple relationship between level of dose and effects. Observation of vascular problems noticed after several accidents in nuclear power stations, including Chernobyl, shows that in all cases the severity of the cases is the same whether the radiation level is 8 or 175 roentgens, 15 or 300, 24 or 400. Quite a range for so-called low levels of radiation! The picture is completely different when we look at high levels. In these cases, the severity of the problems corresponds to a greater extent with the level of radiation the subjects were exposed to.

'The same results were observed in the animal experiments. Even when multiplied by a factor of twenty, the radiation doses always produced the same effects.

'We were able to confirm that low-level radiation combines with other factors in a synergism to exacerbate symptoms. When animals were simultaneously exposed to radiation and any other toxic substance, the combined effect was greater that a simple adding together of the effects of each. If the doses were raised, this was no longer the case.

'Why, then, can people's health deteriorate to such a degree from exposure to only 1 to 20 roentgens of radiation? Thanks to research carried out exclusively on cell membranes, we found that *the body's rehabilitation systems only start to work when exposed to high levels*. Thus, there is a certain threshold below which these systems do not function.

'Our bodies, then, do not possess the ability to adapt to prolonged exposure to low levels of stimuli. That is why the theory by which one sudden dose of a hundred roentgens is more harmful than exposure to a total of a hundred roentgens spread over a year is fully verified. But in the case of a dose of one roentgen spread over a year, compared with a sudden dose of one roentgen, the opposite is true.'

I have allowed myself to quote at such length from Elena Burlakova's report in order not to misrepresent her train of

67

thought by one iota. Nevertheless, according to her own words, these data are only fragmentary and incomplete, and have only been tested on animals. It has also been found that the damage to the membranes was not lethal, but that it altered the body's ability to adapt itself. With what result? It's not smoking which reinforces the effects of radiation, but radiation which reinforces the effects of tobacco. It's not pesticides which reinforce the effects of radiation, but vice versa. And when we are exposed to radiation, we are more vulnerable to other harmful substances in our environment.

It follows then that we can predict that in regions where particular illnesses predominate, exposure to radiation will have a powerful boosting effect on their progression.

Are we in the presence of a new concept? Is this the moment of truth? It is possible, even though, as she has stressed so many times, Elena Burlakova does not consider her theories completely proven. But her scientists had found a way to explain previously inexplicable facts without sensationalism. More experiments will have to be done on animals, and tests will have to be done on people who have been exposed to the radiation, not only those who worked on the reactor immediately after the catastrophe, the so-called 'liquidators' involved in the clean-up operation, but also the people living in the contaminated zones.

What doctors have found confirms the theory proposed by Professor Burlakova. Russian paediatricians whom she told of her conclusions have confirmed that the conditions the children are suffering from could be symptoms of irradiation syndrome.

It has also been found that the Institute of Biophysics of the Ministry of Health of the Russian Federation had in its possession all the data on the effects of the accident on the Techa. Why, then, did Iline and his colleagues not compare them with the data from the contaminated zones after Chernobyl? It was their data, after all.

RIGHT: *A cruciform oak, dried out by radioactivity. During the second world war, partisans were hanged on the branches of this tree and buried underneath: it became a local memorial. A storm has now felled the tree.*

In her quest for the truth, Elena Burlakova needed to go in search of the 'liquidators', those men forgotten by God and Soviet medicine. To do this she had to go to Erevan, to the Institute of Radiology, where the liquidators from Armenia are based. They had come from Erevan to Chernobyl, into a furnace, a hell, to work in peril of their lives! And after it had used them, the State had immediately forgotten them. That's Soviet-style government! Elena Burlakova said that these young men complained of weakness and continual headaches; after just a short walk they were out of breath. But from the official point of view they were faking it. All the hundreds and thousands of them? At Erevan, Narodichi, Kiev, and in Byelorussia? All faking the same symptoms... Why be surprised if, in some contaminated zones, even children with thyroid problems are not followed up as victims of the catastrophe!

Elena Burlakova, like many others, could not understand why in our country, a person who wants to leave one region cannot do just that. She said that in Narodichi a woman had stood up in a meeting to say: 'I don't want money or anything else. Just let me leave. I don't want to live here. Help me leave, to register in a 'clean' area and find work there.' Truly, we live in feudal times! I can understand why people say: 'We are your hostages. We are here, we can't leave, and you come here with your foreign colleagues and study our condition. We won't let you.' And imagine the cynicism needed to reply: 'You want to use evacuation to solve your personal problems.' Professor Burlakova is a sensitive woman, not indifferent to this.

After her trips to the contaminated areas, her 'protégés' started to send letters, poetry, and local papers in Ukrainian. And what letters! She was sent greetings on special occasions, thanks, blessings. With her authorisation, I am going to reproduce an extract from one of these. It's an overwhelming document, sent by people in despair. Professor Burlakova made their suffering her own.

Dear Elena Borissovna,
    We run the Pripyat Association which is an organisation of former inhabitants of the town of the same name. Our

families have suffered the catastrophe, evacuation, and after many incidents, after voluntarily giving up our lodgings in Kiev, we finally settled in Slavutich.

Practically all of us are relatives of people who worked in the Chernobyl nuclear power station before and after the accident, and who continue to work there. Among us are people suffering from irradiation syndrome, there are some who need to be examined and to receive expert care, and there are weak, sick children. Our society was formed in order to unite and support the victims of the accident who are a minority in this town (two thousand people, including children).

We have a constitution, a programme, and a bank account. Our association was formed with a simple, very definite aim. We feel that it is necessary to draw the attention of the Supreme Soviet, the governments of the USSR and the Ukraine, and scientists to our problems.

What we want right now are answers to the following questions: (1) What does the future hold for the former inhabitants of Pripyat after the Chernobyl power station has been shut? (2) How, and by which authorities (Ministry of Health, Nuclear Energy Ministry), will the real doses of radiation that we were exposed to during and immediately after the accident be worked out? (3) If the town of Slavutich was built in a contaminated zone, what are the possibilities of our families returning to Kiev, where most of us had lodgings that we gave up? (4) If we stay on the polluted land at Slavutich, it is imperative that we receive the statutory rights of victims so that we do not have to humiliate ourselves in front of 'commercial bosses' [in order to have 'clean' products] who only know of the accident from newspapers, in front of the administration and the Chernobyl trade union committee.

Our children's state of health requires a balanced diet and holidays, which we are unable to provide for them. Our requests have no support at the Slavutich municipal soviet, since we are so few and because the administration and trade union committee at the nuclear power station are so scornful of us. We are unable to cope with these problems on our own.

How will the question of special pensions as compensation for injuries sustained be sorted out? We passed statistical data and documents about our medical conditions to the Supreme Soviet when we went to Moscow.

Together with Principal Department no. 3 of the Ministry of Health of the Soviet Union, we worked out a programme to record medical developments among our association's members. But, given the state of medical facilities in Slavutich, we have no idea how this can be carried out.

We are also making this appeal to the Council of Ministers of the USSR.

We consider that the fate of the former inhabitants of the town of Pripyat now living in Slavutich should be the subject of a special decree.

This despairing letter was signed by the Chair of the Association, L. Pavlova-Saveleva, and by other members, including V. Sidorov, V. Nosarev, T. Ivashkovich, A. Bogomaz, and O. Koroleva.

All the letters were different: some restrained, others demanding, some begging, sometimes even poetry. Professor Burlakova did not just file them away. She drew out the data from them and translated them into concrete scientific language.

The letter from Slavutich persuaded her to drop everything and go there. Her team set up a base there. People expected answers to precise questions. For example, why had the power station workers' new town deliberately been built in a contaminated zone? At a session of parliament, a representative from the Ukraine Forest declared indignantly: 'When the question of a site for the new town was examined, we opposed the choice that was made. We had various pieces of advice in front of us. It was Comrade Shcherbina, who was the head of the commission, who cut off discussion. What was the result? It is forbidden to collect wild mushrooms and fruit from the forests around the town. This is an established fact, but we accuse the forestry workers, instead of informing the people, of taking down the notices so as not to frighten them. That's the truth.'

Another speaker referred to documents from the State Committee for Hydrology and Meteorology of the USSR, which testified to the level of radioactivity in the town of Slavutich. In the contaminated zone where the town was built, measurements of 0.1 to 4 curies per square kilometre have been recorded, and at some places in the forests up to 19 curies. These figures were known when the site was chosen, and they were confirmed in the following years.

Now, Professor Burlakova and her colleagues, together with those exposed daily to radiation in the comfort of Slavutich, can 'savour' the fruits of irresponsibility bordering on crime against her correspondents from the Pripyat Association, and many others.

Should the theory which she first aired to the government commission be considered a discovery? Many scientists who took part in the debate are convinced it should. By all the evidence, we have just witnessed a moment of truth.

SEVEN

'The greatest catastrophe of our time'

THIS is a disaster of global proportions. That was the conclusion that the State Committee of Experts came to for the first time four years after the drama began. 'The accident at the Chernobyl nuclear power station was, due to its long-term consequences, the greatest catastrophe of the modern era.' What does that mean? The life span of this blue planet is estimated at ten to twelve billion years. More than a third of this has passed. The earth is already aging. And throughout this third of its life there has never been so far-reaching a catastrophe, with such devastating consequences.

The peaceful use of the atom has, admittedly, already brought a few 'annoyances'. In 1979 there was the accident at Three Mile Island, nowadays viewed as an alarm bell, and before and after it twelve less serious incidents at nuclear reactors.

In the Soviet Union we can consider three accidents in 1949 at the Mayak production combine on the River Techa in the Urals to be precursors of Chernobyl. Apart from these, there have been more than ten incidents in nuclear plants around the country. In June 1989 alone, nineteen unplanned shutdowns and partial shutdowns were recorded. Local radioactive pollution was recorded three times after incidents in the reactors at Leningrad, Chernobyl (in 1982) and Kursk. Until recently such information was kept jealously secret by the nuclear lobby.

But all this put together is merely a drop in the radioactive ocean which spread out after the explosion at Chernobyl.

The information on the global catastrophe at Chernobyl contained in the official conclusion of the State Commission of

Experts is overwhelming. The Soviet report presented to the meeting of the International Atomic Energy Agency in Vienna in 1986 confirmed that 50 million curies of various radionuclides have escaped into the atmosphere. In particular, one million curies of radioactive caesium and 0.22 million curies of radioactive strontium were recorded. At the international conference on safety in nuclear reactors which took place at Dagomis in November 1989, some scientists declared that according to their calculations, the level of caesium was even higher. Foreign specialists put forward figures one and a half to two times higher than those of their Soviet colleagues.

According to the estimates of the Research Institute on Nuclear Reactors, the total amount of radioactive released reached a billion curies, while according to some estimates it reached 6.4 billion. The levels of caesium-137 alone were equal to 300 Hiroshimas.

The millions of curies of radioactivity released daily until 9–10 May 1986, the winds which carried the pollution all over the world, the extremely complicated process of 'burning' the radionuclides in the zone around the destroyed reactor, where the temperature reached 2500 degrees Celsius, all led to a catastrophic level of radioactive contamination over immense areas of the country in spring 1986. It was as if the reactor had disgorged the entire periodic table, plus a few other elements unknown to science.

This is the judgement of the chair of the State Committee for the Protection of Nature, N. Vorontsov, on the consequences of the catastrophe:

'In a way, the entire world is in the Chernobyl zone in the wider sense of the term, especially all of the Soviet Union. We have a map of the pollution, and from it we can see that one of the trajectories passes right through the centre of the European part of the Soviet Union, up to the Urals and western Siberia.'

A rise in background radiation was recorded not only in our nearest neighbours, Poland, Romania, Norway, Finland, and Sweden, but even—incredibly—in Brazil, Japan, Austria, Italy, and in other countries. The chair of the State Committee for

75

Hydrology and Meteorology, Yuri Izrael, said:

'The pollution crossed Sweden, Poland, Bulgaria, Germany and England. In the aforementioned countries, the levels of radioactivity are higher than one curie per square kilometre, but only just, it must be said—the figures are 1.2 to 1.5 curies. The map supplied not only by Soviet meteorologists, but also by their colleagues abroad, shows high levels of pollution in northern Italy and Bavaria. Where it rained, the pollution stayed, especially the caesium.'

At a meeting of the Committee for Ecology and for the Protection of the Environment, Yuri Izrael showed a booklet giving wind directions. In it, it was possible to follow the direction of the radioactive clouds hour by hour. 'Look,' said Izrael, 'it is clearly marked. On the 26th at 03.00 and 15.00, and on the 27th at 03.00. Part of the Baltic coast was already affected. But by the night of the 27th, the cloud had reached Copenhagen. At three o'clock on the morning of April 26 we had no idea that it would.' In twenty-four hours, the radioactive 'smoke' had reached the coast of Denmark.

According to data from the State Committee for Hydrology and Meteorology, four regions of Russia, five regions of the Ukraine and five of Byelorussia were submitted to intense radiation. We know that in the first few days after the accident, 116,000 people were evacuated. Around 144,000 hectares of farmland were covered with radionuclides and had to be 'frozen'. These areas are dead.

But how much of contaminated land is still being ploughed, sown and harvested? Up till now, according to official figures, in the three republics 'scattered' with the most active radionuclides—from one to a hundred curies or more—around 10 million hectares of farmland were contaminated by caesium, of which over three million are exceptionally fertile.

In Ukraine, 377,500 hectares of land were contaminated with five curies or more per square kilometre. Plus 3,316,000 hectares with under 5 curies. These were the data presented to the Commission of Experts. According to data from the Department of Radiology of the Ukraine Department of Food and Agriculture, which were supplied to me on request, 7,220,000 hectares of farmland in the Ukraine are contaminated. The areas around Kiev and Zhitomir are particularly badly affected. As the vice-chair of the executive committee for Kiev region, N. Stepanyenko, told me, over 1,600,000 hectares of land in this region have been irradiated. In Zhitomir region, the total area contaminated is 466,700 hectares.

Byelorussia has 7,000 square kilometres of radioactive land. A fifth of all farmland is extremely dangerous to human life. The region of Mogilev was the most tragically affected: it has 1,430 square kilometres of land contaminated by radionuclides.

Russia is a special case. The clean-up operation proposed to the Committee of Experts by the Council of Ministers of the Russian Federation comprised... just one region, Briansk. According to unofficial data, 5,500 square kilometres in seven western regions are contaminated and according to official figures, 1,000. The experts did not mention the existence of the Orlov-Kaluzha-Tula zone, where the level of caesium-137 pollution has reached 5 curies per square kilometre, and as high as 15 in the town of Plavsk in Tula region. The radioactivity extends over 2,000 square kilometres.

In fact, the Council of Ministers of the Russian Federation had not fulfilled the orders of the Soviet government, which were to work out a long-term programme to deal with the effects of the accident in the whole republic. At the session of parliamentary hearings of the Committees of the Supreme Soviet of the USSR on 12 April 1990, the vice-chair of the Commission of Experts, A. Nazarov, a doctor of biology, declared:

'We have heard the statement from Comrade Tabeyev [the first vice-chair of the Council of Ministers of the Russian Federation, and chair of the Commission dealing with the consequences of the accident], and what he said about the programme in the Russian Federation sounded somewhat strange to us. No inquiry, no information on the huge contaminated zone shown on the map supplied by the State Committee for Hydrology and Meteorology, which covers the Tula, Kaluzha and Orlov regions. This question was not considered at any stage, and there is still no programme for the whole of the Russian Federation.'

And that was four years after the catastrophe!

The Commission of Experts notes in its conclusions that the contamination reached the regions of Krasnodar, Sukhumi, and the Baltic countries. The Krasnodar region is the Caucasian riviera on the Black Sea. There are hundreds of coastal resorts, rest homes and holiday camps. That was where I went for a holiday in May 1986 with my children, thinking that for a few weeks at least I would be able to keep them out of the reach of Chernobyl. All these regions were affected by the radioactivity, which is still affecting today the thousands of people who go there from all corners of the country, some of them relatively 'clean', to spend their holidays.

The high number of people living in the zone affected by the radioactivity bears witness to the breadth of the catastrophe. According to official figures, 2,504,000 were affected; unofficial figures put the number at nearly four million. Some even put it above six million.

The genetic base of Byelorussia is on the edge of extinction. As the representative of the Byelorussian Supreme Soviet's Commission for dealing with the consequences of the Chernobyl accident stated at the parliamentary hearings, 'Fate has caused the tragic history of the Byelorussian people to repeat itself. In the second world war we lost one inhabitant in four; in the Chernobyl accident, we are losing one in five.' Five hundred villages were affected in twelve districts of the Mogilev region. A hundred and eighty four are in zones under strict control. Radioactivity levels there are as high as 140 curies per square kilometre. The press has reported the following: in a nursery school in a village in the district of Krasnopol, over 100 microroentgens were recorded on the paving slabs in the playground, over 200 by the sandpit, and 450 on the grass; the maximum permissible level is 20. Nearby, in an orchard, the radioactivity level is as high as 400 curies per square kilometre.

Even if the 35 rem theory was adhered to, the cleaning-up programme in Byelorussia planned to evacuate approximately 22,000 people in the two years 1990-91.

In the Ukraine, according to official data, the population of the contaminated areas is 1,480,000 people. In my capacity as a member of parliament, I composed a written question to the Council of Ministers of the Ukraine about the evacuation of people living in the dangerous zones. The vice-president of the State Planning Committee, V. Popov, replied:

'In 1990-91, we will need to evacuate approximately 45,000 people. To this end the Council of Ministers of the Ukraine has passed two decrees: the first dated 30 December 1989, entitled: "The evacuation of certain localities in Narodichi district (Zhitomir region) and Polyesye district (Kiev region), and the construction of industrial and service buildings", and the second, number 228, dated 23 August 1990, entitled "Organisation of the fulfilment of the decree of the Supreme Soviet of the USSR enti-tled 'Urgent measures for the protection of citizens of the Ukraine against the consequences of the Chernobyl catastrophe' "'.'

It was planned to evacuate more than 20,000 people from the radioactive villages in Zhitomir region to the south of the region. However, these regions comprise 455 localities inhabited by 93,000 people, of which 20,000 are children. We now also have to evacuate the people living in houses built in a zone known to be radioactive. Hundreds of millions of roubles have been thrown out of the window, not to mention the psychological damage, the irreversible effects on the health of thousands and thousands of innocent people.

On whose advice, with whose blessing did all this take place? Who took the decisions? That is what I had been trying in vain to find out since 1987, when I visited the radioactive villages. I have told in the previous chapters how, when confronted with this question, the various levels of the hierarchy passed the buck back and forth. Today I know who was responsible. Their names were communicated to me in response to a written question by the chair of the executive committee of Zhitomir region, A.

Malinovski. The building work, especially in areas of high radiation (from which we are now evacuating people), was undertaken 'in accordance with a decree of the Central Committee of the Communist Party of the Ukraine and the Council of Ministers of the Ukraine'. There were three of these during the autumn. In the following years, there were three other decrees from the Council of Ministers, without the support of the Central Committee. There are also four applications signed jointly by the Regional Committee of the Community Party of the Ukraine and the Executive Committee of the region. According to official figures, 93 families have been evacuated from the dangerous zones to less dangerous ones. It's a crime.

The same criminal situation exists in Kiev region. In over seventy villages, the density of the contamination has reached five curies or more. Polyesye district has suffered particularly harshly. The villages of Yasyen and Shevcheko have still not been completely evacuated. As the Academy member Iline announced to Parliament in April 1990, Yasyen was not due to be evacuated until 1993. What was that to mean for the residents? Even according to official data, they will have been exposed to radiation totalling approximately 35 rems. The executive committee for Kiev region is currently preparing to evacuate only eighteen villages, that is, about 20,000 people.

I have recently learnt that it was also proposed to evacuate six villages in the Roven and Chernigov regions, and that during that fatal spring the contamination also reached the region of Ivan-Frankov.

But it is doubtless the Russians who found themselves in the most complex situation. If rumours were flying around in Byelorussia and the Ukraine, nothing was heard of the contamination in Kaluzha, Orlov and Tula regions. The number of people living in this zone has not been communicated to either the Soviet government or the State Commission of Experts. Only Bryansk region was mentioned. There, the contaminated area contained over 700 villages, home to a fifth of the region's inhabitants. There are nearly 30,000 children in the zone under strict control. Up to April 1990, only 20 per cent of the population of the dangerous zones had been evacuated. The inhabitants of the villages of Zaborye, Bukovets, Kobali, Porki and Nikolayevka, where life has become dangerous, are still there, especially the children, who have already received doses of radiation higher than the limits set by Iline himself.

Recently we gave been hearing of still more affected areas. The Moscow papers published an open letter from the Byelorussian writer Aless Adamovich, a member of the Soviet parliament, to the vice-chair of the Council of Ministers of the USSR, to the chair of the Bureau for the National Grid, B. Shcherbina, and to the minister for nuclear energy, N. Lukonine. He asked the following question: 'Is it true that if the furthest districts of Mogilev from Chernobyl—Krasnopol, Slavgorod, Cherikov, a part of Kostyukovich region, Bikhov, Klimovich and a few others (as well as some districts in Briansk region)—were exposed to quite high levels of radiation, it is because the cloud heading from Chernobyl towards Moscow was bombarded in order to make it "land" in those areas?'

Aless Adamovich is not the only one to be preoccupied by this question. Some scientists are expressing the same possibility. The residents of Mogilev region are also of this opinion.

Is it true? And if it is the case, what would have been the consequences if the cloud had gone further and further ... where would it have 'fallen to earth', in all probability?

This question was also put to the Committee for Ecology and the Rational Use of Natural Resources, during the discussion between the deputies, the experts, and Yuri Izrael. This is the explanation he gave: 'Around 10 May, Nikolai Rizhkov rang me up and told me: Let's try and make sure it doesn't rain in the Chernobyl area. The radioactivity is disintegrating. The most radioactive substances will disintegrate first. We had to send planes into the cumulus layer before it got to Chernobyl to make it rain. We did that from 10 May onwards.

'The Ukrainians and Byelorussians were worried that it might cause drought in their regions. Nikolai Ivanovitch said to me:

"Get on with it, and never mind about the drought." I can confirm once again that our planes only flew in this sector, and that they only attacked "clean" clouds, making it rain wherever possible. The first rain fell on Chernobyl in June, after the end of this operation.'

Izrael denied categorically Aless Adamovich's version: 'Absolutely absurd suppositions are being advanced that we made the cloud "land" in Byelorussia. For one thing, contamination appeared in these areas from the very beginning, and it rained heavily there on 27 and 28 April. If regions further afield were contaminated, such as Tula, Mogilev and Gomel, it's not only because of the rain, but also the fallout...'

Is the story of the radioactive clouds being bombarded false, then? In any case, it is true that if the clouds had not 'landed' on the fields of Byelorussia and the forests of Bryansk, they would have arrived at Moscow. Nobody doubts that. Some solid particles did reach the capital, and were found in people's gardens. It is quite probable that they 'nose-dived' onto balconies, and into open fanlights...

But the global nature of the disaster can obviously not be measured solely by external signs such as the breadth of the area polluted and the number of people imprisoned by the invisible radioactive veil. It is still more important to find out the genetic damage it has caused and will continue to cause for generations to come, to entire nations. Up to now, thanks to the vigilance of our authorities, we do not know the real extent of this. Official medicine offers us examples of the type: 'The application of a variety of measures has brought about a lessening of the total dose of radiation sustained by the population by 2 to 2.2 times that originally expected.' It is not stated what the comparisons are being made against. And the chair of the governmental commission, V. Dogukhyev, confirmed only recently that 'the major demographic indicators—birth rates, death rates, natural growth in the contaminated regions of the Russian Federation, Byelorussia and Ukraine—correspond to the indicators for the country as a whole.' Is this correct? 'The sickness rates for the main classes of disease show an upward modification, particularly for adult and infant mortality in the region of Zhitomir.' This secret verdict was signed by a group of researchers from the Academy of Medicine of the USSR two years ago.

At about the same time, the Ukrainian Minister of Health, A. Romanyenko, declared to the May 1989 plenary session of the Central Committee of the party: 'I can tell you in full responsibility that apart from 209 people, no-one is suffering today from illnesses due to radiation poisoning.'

You have got it all wrong, comrade minister! If Iline's 35 rem theory was inspired by economic motives, this lie of the minister's is purely ideological. There are ancient and solid traditions in this field. Nevertheless, can one continue to lie indefinitely?

A year later, V. Dogukhyev communicated the official figures to the Soviet deputies. He declared that '62 per cent of the people examined had sustained radiation doses of 1 to 5 rems. Out of a million and a half people who at the time of the accident were living in the areas most contaminated by radioactive iodine, of whom 160,000 were children under seven years of age, 87 per cent of the adults and 48 per cent of the children have suffered irradiation to the thyroid of under 30 rems, and 17 per cent of the children had received 100 rems of radiation'.

That is nearer the truth.

But the truth really came out when Iline himself was forced to recognise not long ago that 'one million six hundred children have received worrying doses of radiation, and we shall have to decide what measures to take.'

In some villages in Mogilev and Gomel regions in Byelorussia, the adults had received a total of 400 rems or more. In twelve villages in Narodichi district, more than one microcurie of caesium-137 was measured in the bodies of 400 adults, and one to five microcuries in a few dozen people, among them some children. Is this not fatal for a child's fragile body? There should in fact be no radioactive caesium in the human body. There can be no question of acceptable or temporary levels. We can only speak of inadmissible levels.

Mutant pine trees near Pripyat.

According to the figures given by the Byelorussian Academy of Sciences, there is a noticeable rise in the instances of vegetative vascular dystonia, hypertension, hyperplasia of the thyroid, and other medical problems.

I recently received an answer from the Ukrainian Ministry of Health to a question I asked on the health of the inhabitants of the radioactive zones in Ukraine and Byelorussia. This was after a new minister, Y. Spizhenko, had been appointed. It is true that the minister does not pay much attention to this matter: in fact, he was deputy minister in the dark years when the secret was well kept. This answer is explained by the fact that he had received an order from above authorising him to speak. This is what he wrote:

The number of people recognised as being in good health according to the results of official examinations carried out over three years has, in total, fallen by 27 per cent and, in particular, by 18 per cent among the 'liquidators', by 33 per cent among evacuees and by 47 per cent among residents of the contaminated zones. This effectively shows a deterioration in the health of the groups of people examined.

The main illnesses the adult population suffer from are problems with the respiratory tract, the vascular system, the nervous system, skin problems, glandular problems and tumours. A causal link between the health problems or handicaps and the effects of working on the clean-up of the Chernobyl accident has been established in over 2,000 people.

Another catastrophe which was global in its consequences followed the Chernobyl one: the madness of allowing livestock to feed on fields which had received a shower of radioactive caesium, enough to make the harvest and produce thereof radioactive. When, from spring 1989 onwards, the deputies meeting during the session of the Supreme Soviet of the USSR demanded that all radioactive farmland be frozen before harvest, V. Dogukhyev declared that a solution would be found to this problem. But no solution was found and we are now in the fifth spring of sowing on radioactive soil.

They make a joke of it in the Ukraine: Narodichi district—the most dangerous on the map of radioactivity of all the zones in the Ukraine—won the socialist prize for the first quarter of 1989! In the previous year, they had produced a thousand tonnes more meat than two years ago. Potatoes, vegetables, eggs, and meat were sent not only to other areas in the Ukraine, for example to the miners at Donbass, but also to regions of Moscow and Leningrad and the Central Asian republics.

We have had five years of the PPL and the MPL, that is to say the provisionally permissible limit (in theory for one year at the most, but it has already lasted five years!) and the maximum permissible limit for radionuclide content. The latter is 8 to 9 times higher than the normal level for beef and 5 times higher for mutton and pork. A new term has appeared since Chernobyl: 'equalisation' of internal levels of radioactivity. For example, contaminated meat from Gomel region is sent to Minsk. Even today, the residents of Minsk are getting the same doses of radioactivity as the inhabitants of Gomel. The Zhitomir meat distributors frequently send contaminated meat back to the farms, as it is even higher in radioactivity than the infamous PPL. The zoologist-in-chief of Svitanok collective farm in the north of Narodichi district, V. Puziychuk, wrote an explanatory note: 'In 1988-89, on my request, meat containing high levels of radioactive pollution was recognised as fit for human consumption.'

Elena Borisovna Burlakova told how a highly-placed personage in the old Department of Food and Agriculture of the USSR declared proudly to an assembly of radiobiologists: 'Thanks to the raising of the PPL, the State has saved 1.7 billion roubles!' Saved with regard to what? Its own future?

Five years after the explosion, the State at last opened judicial proceedings.

The Deputy Prosecutor-General of the USSR, V. Andreyev, wrote in a letter:

The Department of Food and Agriculture of the USSR did not ensure strict enough checks for radioactivity, either at the production stage in the contaminated zones or at point of sale, in consequence of which, in the period 1986-89, 47,500 tonnes of meat and 2 million tonnes of milk over the permitted level of pollution were produced in the afore-mentioned zones. A large part of these products was sent out of the contaminated zones of Ukraine, Byelorussia and Russia. For example, 15,000 tonnes of meat polluted with radionuclides were exported from Byelorussia. These circumstances led to radioactive contamination of food products in practically the whole Soviet Union, which could lead to negative effects on the health of the population.

Since the accident, 28,100 tonnes of radioactive meat have been produced in Byelorussia. 4,000 tonnes were buried, 5,000 tonnes were made into animal feed, and 15,000 tonnes were send to fellow citizens via the Federal Fund.

On the official authorisation of the Ministers of the Russian Federation, in 1989 contaminated meat was brought from the regions of Bryansk, Mogilev, Kiev, and Zhitomir to the regions of Archangel, Kaliningrad, Gorky, Yaroslav, Ivanov, Vladimir, and others, as well as the autonomous republics of Chuvashye and Komi.

The Deputy Prosecutor General of the USSR noted that the 'provisionally permissible levels for radioactive iodine content in drinking water and food products' and the Soviet Ministry of Health's 'permissible levels of radioactive matter in food products were set and adopted ten days or more after the explosion, which led to additional intake of radioactivity by the population by consuming food products contaminated by radionuclides.'

Today, are the governments of the republics in a position to make production conform at least to the PPL? Our group of experts found no such calculations in any republic's programme. The Department of Food and Agriculture in Byelorussia had made the following calculations: every year a billion roubles are spent in the republic on making contaminated products harvested from the fields conform to the PPL! And after five years, this sum will have reached three billion roubles. Isn't it absurd? To spend such sums (in our miserable state too) on improving a product you know is contaminated? Where's the point?

The same could be said of the clean-up altogether. 220,000 military chemical warfare specialists were sent to the area. The experts came to the conclusion that there was no scientific basis for the clean-up. The expected result was not achieved. Trenches were dug to bury radioactive soil—800 already in the Ukraine alone—and after a certain period, the radioactive caesium appeared on the surface again. A million roubles were spent every day on the clean-up programme. Today the cost has reached a billion. This is the price of absurdity.

By what scale, in what currency can we measure the lost health of our young people? Collectively, they have received a dose of about a million rems.

At a recent meeting of the Chernobyl Commission of the Supreme Soviet of the USSR, the coordinator of the experts, G. Sakuline, a doctor of chemistry, also spoke of the ineffectiveness of the clean-up operation. The army carried out its orders. Those who gave those orders have to bear responsibility.

The global catastrophe not only wiped out fertile farmland, but also marvellous forests. Millions of hectares were contaminated. The whole world has heard of the 'Russian forests'. They are dead. And what has happened to the wildlife in the zones under strict control? The oaks, pine trees, acacias and other trees have enormous leaves or needles. The inhabitants of Narodichi say that in their vegetable plots they grow giant cucumbers, and that the pumpkins have strange stems.

Mutations have been recorded in small mammals. Already, in the first two years after the accident, the percentage of dead embryos reached 34 per cent (compared with 6 per cent normally). The activity of the bone marrow was affected, as well as the structure of the cells in the liver and the spleen. Some animals had started to lose patches of fur.

Today, the cost of the effects of the global catastrophe at Chernobyl has risen to over ten billion roubles. The cost of the accident at Three Mile Island was 135 billion, and yet the effects were nothing in comparison. After that accident, only a few dozen people received doses of 0.35 rems. We have millions of victims.

The Ukraine and Byelorussia have declared the Chernobyl explosion a national catastrophe and asked for help from the United Nations.

EIGHT

A travesty of standards

THE villagers of Ladizhino in Vinnitsa region probably do not know that God saved them on 15 March 1966. It was on that date precisely that the Energy Ministry of the USSR decided to build the nuclear reactor for the Ukraine near the village of Kopacha in Kiev region, rather that at Ladizhino as originally intended. The Ukrainian Gosplan Committee gave its agreement to the construction of a nuclear power station in the Kiev region, which was named Chernobyl. The decision taken by the Gosplan on 2 February 1967 was endorsed by a decree from the Central Committee of the Communist Party of the Soviet Union and the Soviet Council of Ministers.

That was the beginning. We know the end.

After the first session of the Congress of People's Deputies, a group of MPs, including myself, asked the Prosecutor General of the USSR to open judicial proceedings against the persons who had obstructed openness—*glasnost*—with regard to the consequences of the accident, and had hidden the information from the residents of the dangerous zones. In December 1989 I received a reply from the Deputy Prosecutor-General of the USSR, V. Andreyev. It was a classic bureaucratic reply, always the same camouflage, the same concealing of the global lie at State level. Not a word of the government decrees setting up the regime of secrecy, nor of the administrative circulars in the same spirit, not a word of the millions of people put in danger by constant exposure to radiation. Not a word of the unchecked spread of radioactive radionuclides throughout the country. It was as if all this did not exist. I read the Prosecutor's reply with a feeling of bitterness and despair. Was it really impossible to break the wall of lies? What could I do?

In one paragraph, as a kind of excuse, V. Andreyev wrote: 'The Constitution of the USSR (Article 164) does not accord the Prosecutor the necessary powers to exercise control over the legality of the activities of the Council of Ministers of the USSR and its Commissions.' The same reply—in another context, it is true—was given to me by the Ukrainian State Prosecutor, M. Potrebenko, referring not to the Constitution, but to the Soviet law on the Prosecutor's office. Not believing my eyes, I consulted the basic law and the law on the Prosecutors. It was true. It follows that the government can do whatever it likes, enact decrees, act and give orders not in accordance with the law, and the Prosecutor, according to the law, has no right to interfere. Such sleight of hand!

At the fourth session of the Congress of People's Deputies of the USSR, when the nomination of a new Prosecutor-General, N. Trubina, was being ratified, I asked him what his opinion of the matter was. Trubina explained that the Supreme Soviet of the republic can annul a decision taken by the Council of Ministers. Or the republic's Committee for the Protection of the Constitution. This can declare decisions taken by the Council of Ministers to be unconstitutional.

It would be annoying to remind an experienced lawyer that the Committee for the Protection of the Constitution has only existed at federal level for a short time, and still does not exist in the republics. Everyone knows what there was at the time of Chernobyl. Has it often happened that the Supreme Soviet of the USSR or of one of the fifteen republics has annulled decrees illegally promulgated by its government? I cannot remember such a case. Perhaps Trubina could remember one? Further-more, it is one thing to annul a decree, but do the Supreme Soviets have the right to go further, for example to set judiciary proceedings in motion? Certainly not. The Committee for the Protection of the Constitution of the USSR has no such prerogative. It's understandable. In general, it is extremely convenient that the Prosecutor-General of the USSR has no power to annul a decision or to set legal proceedings in motion. It is doubly convenient that this is not just ratified in a decree or a simple law, but enshrined in the founding principles of the USSR. Was it not for this reason that for nearly four years the Prosecutor-General of the USSR did not breathe a word about the fact that all the information about the consequences of the Chernobyl accident were being kept secret by the government?

In his note, the deputy Prosecutor-General of the USSR, V. Andreyev, blames the underlings, repeating what we all already know, of course, official propaganda having done its job well. 'The consequences were made worse by the concealing of the scale and seriousness of the accident in the first few hours following it. The director of the power station, Bryukhanov, knowingly concealed the high levels of radioactivity, and failed to put into effect measures designed to protect the workforce and the general population. The following have been arraigned: the director of the Chernobyl nuclear power station, V. Bryukhanov, the engineer-in-chief N. Fomine, the deputy engineer-in-chief in charge of Block 2 of the power station, A. Dyatlov, and head of the reactor room, A. Kovalenko, the team leader at the power station, B. Rogozhine, and the inspector at the state commission for nuclear energy, Y. Laoushkine. All were sentenced by the Supreme Court to various terms of imprisonment, and Bryukhanov, Fomine, and Dyatlov were sentenced to the maximum permissible penalty, ten years in prison each.'

The further we get from the catastrophe, the nearer we get, the deeper we delve into the lies. Anatoly Dyatlov, who suffered exposure to nearly 500 rems of radioactivity, spent three years in prison before being released. But that is just a manner of speaking, for there is little chance of his being freed from what has happened, from his terrible thoughts. Anatoly Dyatlov was only released thanks to the intervention of several members of parliament, of Elena Bonner, wife of the Academy member Sakharov, and finally of the President of the USSR.

Today, after nearly five years, not many people will remember that during the judicial enquiry held in summer 1987, a special procedure was set in motion to look into the reliability of the RBMK reactor, which is in use in other power stations besides Chernobyl. This is V. Andreyev's reply to me on that subject: 'The Prosecutor-General of the USSR started a judicial procedure to determine the reliability of this type of reactor; in the course of the enquiry recourse was taken to technical advice from several recognised expert sources in the field of nuclear power. The conclusion was that the technical and safety systems were sufficient to ensure that the reactor should function without danger as long as the correct procedures were followed. The enquiry was then closed, as the accident had been blamed on multiple violations of procedures and safety regulations, in particular the shutting down of several safety mechanisms.' In short, everything was normal.

But was this really the case? After considerable effort, our commission succeeded in getting access to the file on the case (one would have thought it was radioactive too!). After a few days, the Supreme Court asked us to give it back, but the leaders of the commission decided not to comply until we had had time to study it in detail. The Prosecutor-General kindly offered us the help of seven prosecutors.

In this file weighing several kilos 'concerning persons who did not take adequate measures at the right time to perfect reactors of the type RBMK-1000', there are many interesting things. I will just quote a few examples of the experts' questions and answers:

'Did the technical characteristics of the reactor have any bearing on the course of the accident?' The answer: 'Yes. This is also shown in the report of the governmental commission: "The accident which led to the destruction of the reactor followed the course it did because of construction faults in the reactor". The primary cause of the radioactive emissions was water boiling in the active section due to a fault in the construction of the reactor ... The radioactive emissions were not stopped by the safety systems after they had been set in motion. This shows another fault in the safety systems.'

For several months, our commission received a large number of extremely interesting documents covering the second judicial enquiry, which concerned the reactor's construction faults.

We found a specialist from the Kursk power station, A. Yadrikhinski, who six months before the explosion had sent a letter to the State Committee on Nuclear Energy warning about the dangers of the RBMK type reactor, and explaining the need to commission an independent examination of the need to revise the safety systems. He received the following reply: 'These conclusions have no foundation.'

How can we explain this attitude? Through their conviction that they were right? A mistake? Scorn (think a while, a minor retired inspector of nuclear safety, what does he know)?

It is said that no-one can be a prophet in his own country, and yet the terrible prophecy of A. Yadrikhinski came true well before what happened six months later. After the accident, he was sent to the site. He was given access to the documentation and at the groaning reactor he checked his calculations once again. His scrupulous work, contained in a report entitled 'The accident in Block 4 of the Chernobyl power station and nuclear safety in RBMK type reactors', became a kind of myth. Many people have heard of it, but few have read it. An original copy came into the hands of our commission.

On 24 June 1989 a meeting of the Committee for Ecology and Rational Use of Natural Resources of the Supreme Soviet of the USSR was held, during which there was a debate on the election of the chair of a new committee, the state committee to oversee safety in the nuclear industry. The international agreements signed by the Soviet Union in Vienna at the International Atomic Energy Authority stipulate that signatories must have an independent committee to oversee safety in nuclear energy installations.

On 27 February 1990, on a decision of the new committee, a commission was formed to look into the causes and circumstances of the accident in Block 4 of the Chernobyl nuclear power station. Its report, signed by its chair, N. Steinberg, covers nearly eighty closely typed pages. It is an enormous piece of work, but the introduction states that it is not yet complete.

Isn't it strange that five years after the accident, when dozens of seminars and meetings had been held and scientific and technical advice sought, both within the USSR and at international level, and reports had been presented by the Soviet Union to the International Atomic Energy Authority, passions were still running high in the scientific world on the Chernobyl type of reactor? Might it not be because up till now, no scientific publication had dotted the i's properly? It is my personal opinion, as well as that of a number of the members of our commission, that N. Steinberg's report fills that gap.

Everyone was surprised at the results of the analysis of the reports presented by the USSR, on the one hand at the IAEA meeting in Vienna from 25 to 29 August 1986, and on the other hand at the international conference on indicators of nuclear safety entitled 'Chernobyl: one year after' held from 28 September to 2 October 1987. These two reports supported our government's official version, according to which the cause of the accident was 'an unlikely combination of violations of the rules and regulations on the running of nuclear power stations on the part of the staff in the generating block.' And there it ended: full stop.

But—and this fact is of great interest—the report of the Kurchatov Institute of Nuclear Energy, which was adopted *after* the report was presented to the IAEA, said that 'the prime cause of the accident is an unlikely combination of violations of the rules and regulations on the running of nuclear power stations on the part of the staff, *which brought to light the construction faults in the reactor and the safety system*'. The words in italics were not present in the version of the report which was presented to the IAEA. What does that mean? Could there be one version of the truth for export, and another for internal use? This is what Steinberg writes on the subject in his report:

Since May or early June 1986 we had known of the divergence of the RBMK-type reactor from the nuclear industry's safety standards and the technical problems that the project had been having. This information is contained in the reports presented to the government commission, but they were not made available to the scientific community, nor to the public. They are also missing from the material presented to the IAEA. Much earlier, on 24 December 1984, a decision had been taken by the nuclear industry's scientific and technical advisory council to ratify the proposals of its fourth and fifth commissions of experts on partial modifications to the RBMK type blocks then in service to bring them up to safety standards. Unfortunately, the commission did not pay attention to certain peculiarities in the RBMK-1000 reactor which proved to be of utmost importance, both at the start and in the development of the accident on 26 April 1986.

In its report, Steinberg's commission cites dozens of violations of the 'Safety regulations for nuclear power stations' and the 'General rules for ensuring safety in nuclear power stations at project stage, and during design, construction and use'. This is its conclusion:

All the negative characteristics of the type of reactor in question inevitably had to lead to an accident, which demonstrates that what happened was in no way exceptional and did not result from an unlikely combination of violations of the rules and regulations on the running of power stations... The designers of the reactor no doubt understood full well the dangers that could ensue from such conditions, and knew, even before the accident, how to improve safety, as only a month and a half after the catastrophe they enumerated the technical measures that were urgently needed. The very essence of these measures totally contradicts the official version of human error.

How is it that such one-sided information should have been presented to the IAEA? Were there any scientists and specialists who were pointing out the design faults in the RBMK type of reactor? Apart from A. Yadrikhinski, the prophet, after the accident on 5 May 1986 the interdepartmental advisory commission under the new Soviet deputy minister for mechanical construction, A. Meshkov, always maintained the same version.

A week before, on 1 May 1986, the head of safety in nuclear power stations, V. Volkov, had presented to the Director of the Kurchatov Institute of Nuclear Energy his own version of the accident, according to which it had been caused 'not by the staff, but by the defective design of the active section and a lack of understanding of the physical processes which took place there.' On 9 May he sent the same letter to the country's leaders.

A group of specialists from the Soviet Ministry of Energy sent an amendment to the body looking into the accident, concerning the construction faults in the reactor.

Despite the proof demonstrated at two meetings of the inter-departmental scientific and technical advisory council on 2 and 17 June 1986, chaired by the Academy member Alexandrov, these facts were not taken into account as much as they should have been. The causes of the accident were attributed almost entirely to human error. This position became the official one, and it was this which was presented to the IAEA in the name of the USSR.

On 17 May 1989 the *Literaturnaya gazeta* printed an interesting interview by the journalist Igor Byelyayev, called 'Is this the right road?' The interview was with V. Bobrov, acting head of the State Laboratory registering inventions made by the Central Institute for Information on nuclear energy, who explained why the RBMK type reactor had not been entered onto the register of inventions. This had been requested by the director of the Institute of Nuclear Energy, Academy member A. Alexandrov, and some of his colleagues. Bobrov says:

In 1967, I sent back the first application (one and a half typed pages, not including formulae and plans) to the authors for revision. What happened next was difficult to believe. The revised application for the RBMK, dated 6.10.1967, had not yet been examined when, a month later, Academician Alexandrov declared in *Pravda* (in an article entitled 'October

RIGHT: *Young mothers and their babies in a radiation zone in Zhitomir region, 1991.*

96

and physics') that 'scientists have succeeded in solving the problem of raising the economic efficiency of nuclear power stations'. Yet one of the reasons why the application had been refused was precisely the absence of any industrial logic from the method used to reduce the cost of the electricity which meant that the RBMK was going to be operated with an efficiency ratio of around 30 per cent, equivalent to that of the oldest reactors. That is what the author of the project claimed after his forceful irruption onto the nuclear scene in 1973. I remember that it happened at the Leningrad nuclear power station, where several similar incidents later took place which were hushed up. Academician Alexandrov's claim for an 'avant-garde level of technology' in the RBMK reactor has not been verified, so that the State Commission did not award it a patent and did not register it on the list of Soviet inventions.

However, Academician Alexandrov succeeded in imposing his 'baby' on the country on a large scale. From 1971 to 1975, these dangerous reactors constituted two-thirds of the capacity of planned nuclear power stations.

Here is an extract from the report of the Committee to Oversee Safety in the Nuclear Industry in the USSR, entitled 'On the causes and circumstances of the accident on 26 April 1986 in Block 4 at the Chernobyl nuclear power station':

The staff did effectively commit violations of the technical regulations. Some of these had no effect on the course of events, while others occasioned phenomena which were inherent in the design faults of the RBMK-1000. The violations of the rules can to a large extent be explained by the vague nature of the operating rules and by contradictions in them, themselves due to the mediocre quality of the whole RBMK-1000 project. The staff were ignorant of some of the dangerous properties of the reactor, and consequently were unaware of the consequences of their errors. In fact, it is not so much the level of expertise of the operating staff with regard to safety which is in question, but that of the originators of the project and of its rules of operation.

The commission's report cites an interesting fact, the reaction of the originators of the Three Mile Island project to the accident which happened there. They did not attempt to blame the staff in any way, because the engineers 'have to analyse the first minute of the incident for several hours, or even several weeks, in order to understand what happened or advance theories on the evolution of the process in the case of modified parameters.' Edward R. Frederik, the American operator who took the fateful decisions on 28 April 1979, and who was not prosecuted, wrote: 'How I would love to go back in time and change my decisions. But one cannot change what has happened, but it should not be repeated; an operator should never again be in a situation which the engineers have not analysed in advance. The engineers must never analyse a situation without taking into account the reactions of the operator.'

The Steinberg commission concluded that the main cause was not human error, nor was it psychological or professional circumstances. The accident was programmed, perforce. 'The construction faults in the RBMK reactor used in Block 4 of the Chernobyl power station constituted the preconditions for the serious consequences of the accident.' This is the commission's definitive 'diagnosis'.

Will the Prosecutor-General of the USSR reopen criminal proceedings on the safety of RBMK type reactors?

The Chernobyl explosion put a big question mark over the future of nuclear energy. It set off a whole wave of anti-nuclear movements in western countries. The 'green' parties were strengthened by it.

Professor Pellerin, from France, came to Zhitomir region, to Narodichi. This is what the Chair of the Executive Committee of Narodichi District, V. Budko, had to say at a round table discussion organised by the *Moscow News*: 'Professor Pellerin visited us at Narodichi, and when I told him that we divided the villages into "dirty" and "clean", and therefore that uncontaminated products were delivered to some and not to others, he was astonished and asked me three times via the interpreter if it was true that people living in an area where the level of radiation exceeded 100 curies per square kilometre were not provided entirely with "clean" produce. He could not believe it.' The press did not report that.

The visits of foreign specialists to the radioactive regions of Ukraine and Byelorussia unleashed a new flood of lies in the local press. On 7 August 1989 *Radianska Zhitomirshchina* published a 'scoop' interview with the director of the radiological clinic at the Federal Centre for Atomic Medicine at the Ukrainian Academy of Medicine, V. Bebyeshko. Its title was 'Radiation and health', with an eloquent subtitle: 'The conclusions of WHO experts agree with the opinions of Soviet medical researchers'. It is easy to understand why Bebyeshko and no-one else was interviewed: his position is well-known. Today it is unbearable to read this article.

How can one not agree with the opinion expressed by Professor A. Mishchenko from Moscow University at a press conference on 8 February 1991 on the theme, Ecological disasters: events, causes, and consequences: 'The government calls in foreign scientists when their Soviet colleagues do not agree with government projects. They look for more docile advisers, and they find them abroad.'

Lately, we have been hearing more and more talk of a 'nuclear mafia' or a 'nuclear lobby', in various contexts. Professor Burlakova is convinced that 'nuclear medicine was a political science,' and that 'there is a radiological lobby. Medicine which treats the consequences of the nuclear industry is in the hands of a lobby whose aim is not to protect people, but to promote nuclear energy.'

Recently, in a new inter-republic newspaper called *Nabat* (Alarm Bell) published by the Byelorussian writer Vasil Yakovenko, there was an article by Alexander Lyutsko, holder of the Chair of Nuclear Physics at the University of Byelorussia, recounting events at the heart of the IAEA itself. 'Samples of soil and food products which I brought from Byelorussia, and whose levels of radioactivity I had already tested, were suddenly "secret".

100

After consultations with the agency's senior management, the director of the laboratory, Robert Danezi, seemed highly embarrassed when he told me that the IAEA was requesting me not to ask for the results of these specimens, as the agency did not wish to be implicated in any possible political use made of them...' That's all we hear!

Alexander Lyutsko spoke of the atmosphere of secrecy created at the request of our government around the international experts looking into the consequences of the Chernobyl accident. The director-general of the agency, Hans Blix, had prepared a memorandum to this effect, which had been pinned up 'last autumn on all the doors at the IAEA laboratory at Zeiberdorf, near Vienna.'

Now that the work of the independent commission of international experts is finished, we can understand why they were surrounded by such secrecy. As the Ukrainian and Soviet member of parliament Vladimir Yavorivskiy, chair of the Ukrainian parliamentary commission on the Chernobyl catastrophe, declared recently on Ukrainian television, the experts had taken away the basis for practically all the laws recently adopted by the Ukrainian Supreme Soviet concerning the contaminated areas and the victims of the accident. One question comes to mind: was it a commission of experts, or a lesson in diplomacy for our government, which is so guilty towards the victims? What role did the 'independent commission of experts' play?

The Chernobyl disaster rebounded like a boomerang on the Soviet nuclear energy industry. What state is it in? Should it continue to run, and if so, in what form? This is an important issue, which should be dealt with separately, and above all by specialists. As for me, I will allow myself to give my opinion, which is shared by some specialists and members of the Soviet parliament. They have all expressed their worry at a parliamentary session which heard accounts of the various incidents which have happened in nuclear power stations. V. Malishev, the candidate for the post of chair of the new committee to oversee the nuclear industry, declared that:

Analyses have revealed 24,500 cases of violations of operating regulations in nuclear power stations. Two thousand four hundred people were involved. The committee only oversees civil reactors. But there are also over seventy research reactors, of which only fourteen will be under the committee's jurisdiction. The others have their own control networks. Furthermore, there are fourteen reactors of the same type as Chernobyl still in use in the country. What should we do? ...

The reactors now being built comply with international standards, but in general safety levels are lower in the USSR than in the developed capitalist countries. Why is this? Because we started to build nuclear power stations without corresponding safety guidelines. We built sixteen first-generation reactors without protective shells. These reactors have no safety systems of the required quality. What was the problem? The fact that most research, design and operating studies consider that it is possible to continue operating these reactors for their intended life, which is thirty years. That means that those which entered service in 1980 will continue in use until the year 2010.

We suggested closing down all these reactors by the year 2000. But the criteria for closure will depend on the modernisation plans put forward in 1989. Taking into account safety conditions, we will have to check the state of the reactors, whether they conform to the new standards, and how far they are from centres of population. I imagine that we will have to consider seriously closing two reactors: Blocks 1 and 2 at Leningrad, and Blocks 3 and 4 at Voronezh. This will be decided by considering all the arguments and the safety conditions in these reactors.

I must say that nowadays we are just as worried by poor quality projects, which pose serious design problems.

A programme of quality assurance is to be put in place as from January 1990, and from 1991 operating regulations will include points on shutting down the reactors, burying waste,

102

etc., which do not exist at present...

All that I shall say on underground nuclear power stations is that they have much higher safety levels. I shall propose that documents be prepared on this subject, which can serve as a basis for discussion.

Now to the opinion of N. Usilina, member of parliament:

The residents of Gorky have signed a petition to stop the nuclear power station there from going on line. There is no total guarantee of safety for a population of three million people. This power station constitutes a threat to the population, it risks putting dozens of enterprises out of business, and it threatens to pollute the Volga basin.

In Semyonov district, in Gorky region, where waste is buried, people are suffering from poor health, especially the children. My constituents are asking when all this is going to stop.

Yuri Izrael, Chair of the State Committee for Hydrology and Meteorology, said:

We are currently examining new safety regulations for the construction of nuclear power stations, which clearly state the minimum radius from a reactor within which it is forbidden to work. Secondly, we should look at concrete situations. For example, I consider that safety in nuclear power stations should be at the highest level, whatever the cost to the State. The main idea is this: the worst accident to date was not at Chernobyl, but at Three Mile Island. But the reactor was encased by a protective shell, and everything that came out of the reactor stayed within the protective casing. The shell cracked, but very few radioactive elements escaped. Nevertheless, more radioactive elements came out of the reactor itself than at Chernobyl. That is why we must build protective casings and bury our nuclear power stations.

Now listen to Aless Adamovich, member of parliament:

Academician Legasov told me that according to his calculations, it was the Armenian power station which would blow up first. I discussed this with him. He gave me a list of the probable order in which power stations would blow up next. I asked him if other scientists knew this. He said yes. And why do they keep quiet? He replied that it was because of clan interests. Very powerful interests.

These ideas were expressed in an interview with the Academy member Sakharov in 1989. I would like to end this chapter with Sakharov's own opinion:

Alternative energy sources, 'clean' ones, cannot at present compete from an economic point of view with polluting energy sources, nor even with hydro-electric power stations. This situation will probably continue for a long time. Obviously things are changing all the time. Nuclear energy is currently more expensive than conventional sources of energy, but oil and gas reserves are running out. Coal is very harmful ecologically: all the types of thermal power stations contribute to the greenhouse effect. Apparently, nuclear power will have to play an increasingly large role in the future, at least for a relatively long period which is all we can make technical prognostications for at present. Obviously we will have to make sure that all necessary safety precautions are taken. There are various ways of achieving this.

Above all, the nuclear reactor will have to be perfected. There are water reactors, where there is nothing to burn; gas-cooled reactors where no explosive mixture is formed; reactors in which, at the slightest incident, the level of radioactivity goes down. All this is possible in theory. And yet there is no 100 per cent guarantee. For example, the threat of terrorist attacks, or missile attacks from the air, exist as long as we live in today's world... My conclusion is as follows: the fundamental decision to be taken on safety is to bury the nuclear reactors.

But can we ensure that burying radioactive elements—with a life thousands of years longer than the power stations themselves—would not pose serious problems for us, our children, our children's children, and thousands of generations to come?

One thing is certain: having survived Chernobyl, humankind will continue to weigh up the relative values of Life and the Reactor for a long time yet.

NINE

Korosten, Lugini and elsewhere

SEVERAL years after the disaster at Chernobyl, I decided to visit the radioactive villages in my region once again. If there were just a few dozen at the beginning, now they are counted in hundreds. Some of them are barely on the map. In general, they are isolated villages surrounded by forest on all sides. It sometimes seems to me that civilisation has not yet reached them. What has changed there in the years since the accident?

It was only after three years, on 1 June 1989, that the village of Voronevo, in Korosten district, learnt that it was in an area of high radioactivity, and that the inhabitants started to receive a salary supplement of 25 per cent. Three years!

In the centre of the village, near the village store, we measured the level of radioactivity at ground level with representatives from the local authorities. The gauge showed 0.112 milliroentgens an hour. In the air one metre above ground level, the level was 0.046. The normal level for these regions is 0.015 to 0.017. Peasants gathered around us, adults and children. I asked them about their life and their health.

Valentina Petrovna Bekh, a cleaner at the village school, told me: 'My son, Vova, is seven. He is often ill, he has a heart flutter. He has just had bronchitis. My daughter, Tanya, is ten. Since the Chernobyl explosion, she has had constant nosebleeds, and she also has headaches all the time.'

They confirmed that there wasn't even a village nurse, no pharmacy, and no communications with the district capital!

The vegetables growing in the kitchen-gardens were contaminated, and also the milk. The village shop had nothing. 'They have sold pork twice. The children are entitled to a tin of condensed milk. We should also have corned beef, but there isn't any. Juice is sold in three litre cartons. There is no baby food.'

The residents of another village under strict control, Obikhodi, were in the same situation. This village has been on the list since 1986—May Day, in fact. At the village shop, the story was the same. The same tears from the mothers. 'The commissioners say: wash twice a day, and you will survive. They also recommend that we boil our potatoes twice. We don't get the "coffin allocation"'.

I asked if there was a hospital at Obikhodi. They showed it to me. We approached the hovel which bore the name. The administration has complained that there is no money for renovation work. Opposite, we could see the flamboyant new building of the village soviet. The Soviet administration knows well the old adage 'Charity begins at home'. The regional authorities have the same policy. The former chair of the regional executive committee, V. Yamchinskiy, showed me an album full of colour photos of magnificent buildings belonging to soviets in different villages. A 'central' newspaper even published an article on this practice in Zhitomir region in times of economic stagnation.

There were old people there, in miserable 'wards'. But with a view of the new soviet building. One of them said bitterly: 'Our farm buildings are better than this hospital. At least there are tiles on the floor!'

The chair of the district executive committee showed me a list of 'buildings to be constructed (some to be refurbished) to satisfy the socio-cultural development needs of the village of Obikhodi, Korosten district'. That sounds good! Real socialist policies! What was needed for Obikhodi's 'socio-cultural development', then? 'A club with room for three hundred people. A hospital with twenty-five beds. A bridge over the River Oleshnya. A 47-km water conduit. Road resurfacing for 45 km. Baths. A park for the tractors. 450 houses to be connected to mains gas. Refurbishment of the livestock farm. A heating plant. Re-thatching of 103 houses.' And so on.

107

Fourteen points in all. Truly, every cloud has a silver lining.

We toured the village streets to measure radioactivity levels. We were advised to start in the courtyard of Natalie Grishchenko, a mother of two. The gauge registered 0.150 milliroentgens in the courtyard. Next to the chair of the village soviet's house, the level was 0.117.

The average level of soil contamination at Obikhodi was 22.6 curies per square kilometre.

It was the end of August, and it was hot. The roads were rutted. Children were playing in the sand. There were 130 of them in the village.

Four years later, it was announced that Obikhodi would probably be evacuated ...

M. Ignatenko, chair of the executive committee of Korosten district, told me: 'We don't even have any means of measuring the levels of radioactivity. Not a single geiger-counter in the whole district. The people at Narodichi have lent us two. Five commissions have been to measure the background gamma radiation here. In 32 places the milk is contaminated. In twelve, there are more than 15 curies per square kilometre. But there are only two villages, Voronevo and Obikhodi, which get milk and meat. And then, not in sufficient quantities. For example, in the third term of the year, Voronevo needed 660 kilos of meat, and only received 209. They needed 870 kilos of poultry, and only got 80. The milk comes from Kiev: the delivery is 100 tonnes short every day.'

Mikhail Fedorovich leafs though some papers: he has sent letters to all levels, from the regional authorities to Gorbachev. With just one request: 'include on the list of places under strict control...', 'send "clean" products, milk, cream, cream cheese, sugar, fish, meat, vegetables... Install gas. A hospital. Send some geiger-counters.' In short, everything. As if no-one had lived here before. Perhaps they really weren't alive?

A. Gutyevich, deputy chief medical officer at the district central hospital, said 'We are in a unique situation: a polyclinic at the district capital, and a hospital at Ushomira, with 25 kilometres

108

between the two. The neurological centre is in the village of Bekhi. The hospital at Ushomira was built in 1902.'

The residents of the area told us that during the second world war, the building was used as a stables. There are now eight to ten patients in each room. The premises are in such a bad condition that the maternity and surgical wards and the casualty department had had to be closed.

Eight kilometres from the polyclinic, in the village of Grozino, a new building project was under way, a magnificent municipal building. This one was destined for the administrative centre of the institute for research into the area of non-black earth in the Ukraine ...

In all the contaminated regions which I have visited at different times, the people wanted income supplements, 'clean' food, and to be put on the list for evacuation. But in one village, there was a different request. This was Bekhi. There, hundreds of people came to meet me, not talking about meat or money. They asked only one thing, that they should be given back their church which had been confiscated by the authorities before the war.

Several years after the accident, it turned out that things were no better in the district capital, Korosten. 'Suddenly' places appeared in streets and courtyards, where the level of radioactivity was extremely high, 100 or even 200 curies per square kilometre. The title of an article by the deputy editor of *Radianska Zhitomirshchina*, S. Tkach, 'A zone which is attracting particular attention', seemed, two years after it came out, to have a sinister irony.

The sequel to my visit to the radioactive villages, which led me now to the district of Lugini, was just as sad. Out of forty-nine places, twelve had been put in the 'strict control' category. Two villages had been included on this list after a year and a half, and the others only in 1989 and 1990. My first stop was the village store in the 'severely irradiated' village of Moshchanitsa. Speaking to the people there, we heard the same complaints as in other villages in other districts. The problems were the same everywhere.

Raisa Ivanovna Demchuk, the shop manager, told us: 'Everyone says that they don't feel well. The authorities want to do some building work here, including road-building, but I think it would be less expensive to evacuate us. All the young people are for it, but the old people are against it. But we have a lot of children aged about 10 and 11. They had a medical check-up at school, but no recommendations were made. We aren't told anything.'

The villagers advised us to measure the radioactivity near the Kobilinskis' house. A newly tarmacked road led to it. It had just rained.

We arrived in front of a large, solidly built house. We pushed open the gate. A path led to the house. On each side were immense mallow bushes with pink and red flowers. The owners of the house came to meet us, and we explained who we were and why we had come.

Vasili Fedorovich Kobilinski, who was retired, told us: 'We have children and grandchildren, but at the moment they don't come to visit us very often. They're afraid. For the time being, we have all we need to live on, but our health is not very good. In the morning I feel as if I am suffocating, I can't speak, I have something in my throat.

'We have had analyses done of the soil, and also of the beetroots, potatoes and onions. We have had everything analysed. But we weren't told what we can eat and what we can't. We eat everything, because we haven't got anything else but what we grow ourselves.

'We were given counters to wear. They came to take them back, but we haven't been told the results. The soil next to the water-trough has been de-activated. The earth was taken away down to 10 or 25 centimetres. But after a while the radioactivity level came up again.'

He led us to his kitchen-garden, behind the barn. We measured the radioactivity where earth had been taken away. On the ground there were 0.175 milliroentgens an hour. One corner of the garden had not been planted. There stood a few silver birch trees, with grass and a small glade. A pile of dried hay. We measured 0.705. In the courtyard, there was some corn: 0.110.

As we were leaving, we measured the ambient radioactivity one metre from the ground: 0.075, five times the normal level. Yet there are people who live there, and life goes on.

We stopped the car after Moshchanitsa and went into a forest heavy with the scent of pine needles and dried leaves. It was hot, the middle of August. Birds were singing. Everything seemed normal. We put the counter on the ground, under a tree: after forty seconds the reading was 0.106. We took two more measurements, with the same result. The forest was dangerous for human life.

The representative from the district executive committee told us that before, wood from this forest was exported. Now, the buyers demand a certificate because of the radioactivity. 'Although there are three thousand hectares of forest in the district, we can't cut a single branch...'

Further on, our route took us through one more chosen village, Malakhovka. At the entrance to the village we saw a monument on our left. A granite slab bearing the portrait of a young man and an inscription: 'This square bears the name of A. Martinchuk, killed whilst carrying out his internationalist duty in the Democratic Republic of Afghanistan'.

Next to the monument we measured the radioactivity in the grass—0.110—and in the air—0.050 milliroentgens an hour.

Opposite the monument was a beautiful garden.

It was impossible to find another place to meet: we were already in the centre of the village, next to the village store.

We met Tamara Alexeyevna Gerasimchuk, the school cook. 'It's the children who are the most sensitive to the radiation. I've got three. The youngest, who is four, has 0.64 microcuries of caesium in his body, the oldest one microcurie. He was sent to Odessa, to the Youth Guard hospital. He was analysed again, but we weren't given the results. Two hundred children are examined every day. If we ask questions, they aren't answered.'

Lidia Afanasyevna Glyevchuk, head librarian, said: 'I'm from

Lipniki, but I work here. My little boy is eleven, he has a swollen thyroid gland, and he also has a liver complaint. He often has attacks at school. When they call the register, there are always a few who are off sick.'

Grigoriy Grigoryevich Vlasyuk, director of the Lipniki state farm: 'There are four villages in our state farm. Two are under strict control, Moshchanitsa and Malakhovka, and two 'normal' ones, Osni and Lipniki. It's only two kilometres from Malakhovka to Osni. The fields are divided by a stream. On the one side, people are paid an income supplement, but not on the other. But the dust doesn't see the difference, it blows onto both sides. At Moshchanitsa the milk is contaminated, we can't sell it any more. People don't have any interest in life. They are often ill, and complain of pains in their joints.

There are eighty-one families in Moshchanitsa. I think the village ought to be evacuated. The radioactivity level is higher than in the 30 square kilometre zone. The caesium level is as high as 30 curies per square kilometre. The map appeared after I had made a fuss at the Ukrainian Department of Food and Agriculture.'

We went to Lipniki, where the headquarters of the state farm is. It was a nice-looking village, drowned in flowers. The roads were tarmacked, there was a wonderful café and a canteen. Everything was produced on the spot, so prices were low. The workers did not complain about living conditions, but they were worried about the radioactivity.

They told me that the chief medical officer at Lipniki hospital, I. Nyevmerzhitskiy, had spoken up in front of the Lugini district soviet—and after a few days a Department of Health commission had come to discipline him. What was his crime? He had told the truth about his patients' health. He had expressed his defiance of official medicine and proposed that a holiday village be built for children near Moshchanitsa or Chorvonoi Voloka, along the lines of Artyek, by the Black Sea. He also took the opportunity to ask the representatives of the Ukraine Ministry of Health some 'difficult' questions: 'Can anyone live at Moshchanitsa, where the

112

The evacuated town of Pripyat, 1991.

ambient level of radioactivity is between 340 and 1,500 micro-roentgens an hour? Are those in charge—or rather in mischarge—right to raise the maximum permissible level of radionuclides daily? Why are the people who died after the bombing of Hiroshima and Nagasaki called victims of American aggression, but when someone dies of cancer in our zone, it has nothing to do with radioactivity?'

The chief medical officer and his patients are still waiting for answers to these questions.

On the road from Lipniki to Lugini, we were 'intercepted' by Nina Ivanovna Danilyuk, the director of the Ostapovskiy state farm. And although we did not have much time—we had to get to the district executive committee and various other administrative offices—we couldn't refuse to meet the people of this farm.

The director, Nina Ivanovna Danilyuk, told us: 'We are in ideal

113

surroundings, so pure and clean, and everyone says how healthy we are. But if that is right, how come thirty-seven people out of fifty examined are suffering from hyperplasia and thyroid problems? Thirteen of our children are in hospital in Kiev, at the national radiation centre. Do they admit people who are in good health? There are also seventy adults on the list for treatment there. We were examined for caesium in our bodies. The examinations took place in two rooms. First I took my daughter Galina into one of the rooms, and they found 0.9 microcuries of caesium, then into the other room where they found 0.1. The third time they found 0.57. What are all these tests for?

'Our milk is contaminated. And there isn't a nursery in the village. The children go to the fields with their parents. Here is the examination report for the fields. We are forbidden to pasture our dairy cattle on the fields marked, where the caesium level is over a certain level, as shown. In all we have 139 hectares of pasture. If we follow these recommendations, we will only be able to put the cows on 25 hectares. We put them out everywhere. What else can we do? At Urochishchye Staritsa, the radioactivity level is 36 times higher than normal. At Krugloye it is eight times higher.

'In the whole of my district, we were made to sign an undertaking not to drink our milk. At Ostapi too. We can't drink it and we can't give it to our children. Each head of family signed. Twice we had to give our signatures. But we don't get any "clean" products, neither milk nor meat.

'We use wood for heating. The wood is contaminated. They ought to install gas and mains water. We are brought wood from the quarry at Jerevtsy. But Zherevtsi is a village under strict control.

'We need 'clean' products, especially the children, and the other benefits too: holidays, income supplements. We haven't had a school built, nor a bath-house. We have no soap or washing powder. Where can the machine operators wash? And the families?'

We then heard from Valentina Ivanovna Primyenko, chair of the Ostapi village soviet: 'For several years we were told that

114

everything was fine here, that the levels were low. Why, then, have I got a prescription for anti-cancer treatment in my hand? Why is my eight-year-old son constantly in hospital? Why have his lymphatic glands swollen up? He has lost 70 per cent of his vision. Who is going to answer for that?'

After our visit to the contaminated villages, we went back to Lugini. At the district executive committee I was told that until 15 June 1989(!), there had not even been a map of the contamination in the district. How could the state farms avoid ploughing fields contaminated with caesium? The agronomists assured them that if they carried out their recommendations, they would be able to obtain 'clean' products from contaminated soils. It is possible. But someone would need to show us the steps to follow in order to apply the proposed technology without a map of the contamination!

Nadyezhda Pavlovna Kovalyeva, director of the veterinary laboratory at Lugini, said: 'On the orders of the regional food and agriculture department, I take samples for radiological analysis. We are never told the results. Twice Loshchilov, the head of the Institute of Radiology at Kiev, has come to take samples of milk, soil and fodder at Ostapi. We still don't know the results of the analyses.

'I have been told that at Kiev the milk is divided into several categories according to temporally permissible levels of radiation. The 'cleanest' goes to Moscow, the 'slightly dirty' goes to Kiev, and the 'dirtiest' is for Zhitomir.

'According to the studies carried out by the Lugini epidemiological centre, a large proportion of wild fruits, almost half of the medicinal herbs, over half the fish, the dried mushrooms, and two thirds of our honey are over acceptable levels. I have also been shown the results of the tests done by the Lugini veterinary centre. Nearly all the samples are over the short-term permissible levels.

'When I examined these documents which burned my conscience, I remembered that during a meeting of the governmental commission with the inhabitants of the northern part of the district, one of the desperate mothers said, with tears in her eyes:

'When I found my five-year-old son by the milk jug, he begged me, frightened, "Please, mummy don't scold me, I didn't drink any milk, I only put my finger in it…" '

For long years, the doctors in charge were in no hurry to let the population know the results of their tests. Sometimes it took a year to 'extract' them from Kiev. In fact, the tests were carried out more to allay people's fears than to provide proper care. Sometimes two hundred children were examined in one day. The medical infrastructure could not cope with serious testing: the zones under 'strict' control only had one ill-equipped hospital for a population of 5,000.

Three years after the accident, the results of the tests on 5,000 children shocked the population: the cases of thyroid problems and circulatory problems had risen by a third, blood disorders by a half, and so on. And in this catastrophic situation, the district had been ordered to implement a plan to collect 260 litres(!) of donated blood a year. Who could they take this blood from, and who could they give it to? It was completely mad. Mad and cruel.

In a report on radioactivity in the district, edited by the head of the Centre for Nuclear-related Ecological Problems at the Ukraine Academy of Sciences, V. Chumak, and the head of research, N. Byelusova, the following sentences can be read: 'The maximum possible dose of radioactivity for the population [of Lugini district] caused by the consumption of local food products could reach ten rems a year. Radioactivity from outside sources… could reach 0.8 rems a year. Given that it takes seven to ten years for soils such as those in the Lugini district to cleanse themselves by 50 per cent, it cannot be expected that the levels of radioactivity will lessen in the short term.'

In the years following the Chernobyl disaster, over 300 letters, telegrams, complaints and declarations were sent to anyone in authority in the district. A citizens' action group sent a hand-delivered, despairing letter to V. Shevchenko, then chair of the praesidium of the Ukrainian Supreme Soviet, and to V. Masol, chair of the Council of Ministers of the Ukraine. 'A month later,' S. Vasilyuk, a manager in the Food and Agriculture department, told me, 'a KGB agent came to test the radioactivity and the morale of the residents.'

Three years after the accident, I got a letter from Kiev, sent by A. Pokreshchouk, a lawyer and professor at the Ukraine Party College. This is an extract from it: 'On 21 June, I was present at a session of the Lugini district soviet. On the next day, I was called to the college urgently. The principal told me that the Zhitomir Region party secretary had phoned to tell him that I was stirring up the population of the district. [Although the secretary wasn't at the session.] It was suggested that I tender my resignation on personal grounds, aggravated by my stance. I refused. So the principal asked me to write a note explaining my actions. I am enclosing a copy...'

The explanation was addressed to I. Grushchenko, principal of the college, and P. Skripki, secretary of the party committee, from the holder of the Chair of Public Law. Strangely enough, there was no hint of an apology, nor a request for reconsideration. He declared that he had been officially invited to Lugini and that he 'had participated in the planning of the meeting', and that he had 'furthermore proposed to the producers of the Ukrainian television programme "My Land" that they make a programme on it.'

I contacted Professor Grushchenko, the principal of the Party College. 'In fact,' he told me, 'V. Kavun, the first secretary of the regional committee, rang me to say that during the session, Pokreshchuk had sown panic and increased tension, instead of helping people. I asked the regional committee to send me an objective description of events. I have now received it, and the party cell will examine his conduct at the session.'

In his letter to the principal, the secretary of the Zhitomir Region Party Committee, V. Kobilyanski, explained that 'in his speech, Pokreshchuk shed no light on the situation, he criticised the work of party organisations and the soviets, he made unwarranted remarks about the leaders of the republic, and he proposed to send a film to the Second Congress of People's Deputies of the USSR.' And as a conclusion: 'These declarations in no way contributed to a normalisation of the atmosphere in the district

117

... and provoked malcontent among the populace.'

But the anger of the authorities did not only fall on Pokreshchuk. The district leadership also received a few thunderbolts. Had such a thing ever been seen before? They had decided to hold a session without the permission of the hierarchy! And what is more, they had devoted it to that which had been so carefully hidden from the public, the consequences of the Chernobyl accident! And to cap it all, they had brought along an expert from Kiev, a television crew, and representatives from four other districts! The regional executive committee had telephoned several days before the session to ask that it not be held. Afterwards, the chair of the district executive committee had been called to a 'strong-arm' meeting with the chair of the regional executive committee to explain things. The regional party committee had been called on to ask what Pokreshchuk thought he was doing.

It was not the levels of radioactivity or the health of the people which was worrying the party bosses. No member (!) of the regional executive had bothered to visit. No, they had other concerns: to prevent any sign of *glasnost*. Punish the troublemakers!

The debates in the 'unauthorised' session of the Lugini district soviet of people's deputies had been broadcast into the street by loudspeaker. People had come to listen. Not one of the four hundred seats in the hall was empty, although there were only 75 deputies. For the first time in the region, two important decisions had been taken. Firstly, a letter had been sent to the Prosecutor-General of the USSR demanding that the Soviet Energy Ministry be prosecuted. Secondly, the amount of damages claimed by the district after the accident was made public: 1,314,630 roubles.

Those who had so carefully hidden the truth from their own people could be satisfied to hear the deputies speak openly over the microphone and in front of the cameras at the 'rebel' session, as the residents had named it.

S. Rashevskiy, first secretary of the party district committee and a deputy (council member), told us: 'Thirty per cent of the district has already been placed under 'strict control'. But the situation is no better in the other districts and villages. Even at Lugini, there are places where the gamma background radiation reaches 0.32 milliroentgens. "There is practically no place"—I am quoting an expert from the Nuclear Experimentation Institute of the Ukraine Academy of Sciences—"where the level of caesium in milk is lower that the provisionally permissible level, in both the private and the state sectors, and in some areas, the radioactivity is ten times or more higher than the permissible levels." The children of Rudnia Povch have been exposed to levels of radiation far higher than those in Ovruch district... The commission which was sent tried to prove that everything was well in the district and that we were as healthy as in a spa resort. The Ukrainian Minister of Health, A. Romanyenko, with whom we have on numerous occasions raised the question of the state of health of the local population, also adopted an incomprehensible position. He has constantly claimed to be ignorant of the true situation and to believe that there is no threat to the health of the population. The leaders of our republic, V. Masol and V. Shevchenko, also show no sign of worrying about the life and health of our children in this complex situation.'

The mistakes which were made in Narodichi district are being repeated in Lugini. This was also openly mentioned during the session. Millions of roubles have been granted to the district to deal with the consequences of the disaster. At Malakhovka, a village under 'strict control', there were plans to build a health centre, baths, metalled roads. At Moshchanitsa, which only has eighty-one houses, they are putting in running water and new fences. Why? Why put money into villages under 'strict control'?

S. Kobilinskaya, infant teacher at Moshchanitsa, asked us: 'What do we need with a road, baths, running waster and gas, when in a few years, and even in one year, no-one will need them? This money could have been used to evacuate people. Because everyone living in our village has health problems. It's impossible to live here. A commission came from Kiev and said that the level of radioactivity was higher in our village than in the thirty kilometre "dead zone". And near the club, it's 2.1 milliroentgens an hour.'

According to P. Kravchuk, tractor driver at the Ukraine collective farm, and a member of the district soviet, 'None of the leaders
of the republic made a single mention of Chernobyl at the first
Congress of People's Deputies. They had a lot of worries: what
insignia the representatives from the Baltic states should have on
their jackets, building a hospital at Yakutiy, how to organise the
militia in Georgia, tracts in support of Gdlyan and Ivanov [judges
recalled for attacking the Uzbek mafia] slipped under hotel
bedroom doors. It seems that in our republic there is no problem
worthy of attention. Of all the republics represented at the
Congress, ours was the one with the fewest problems!'

P. Kozel, chief medical officer at the Chernobyl area hospital,
told us: 'The relevant spokespersons for the health sector assured
us that we had nothing to fear for our future, that the air we were
breathing was pure. Then we were called panic-spreaders, 'radio-
phobes'. But what do we see today? That we were simply
deceived. We can now see that 70 per cent of our children are
suffering from changes in their thyroid glands, whereas in the
general population the normal proportion is six per cent... I only
learnt recently that there was an extraordinary commission set up
by the regional executive committee. If it had done its work properly, we would have known that we shouldn't have picked
mushrooms or herbs, or warmed ourselves with wood from our
forests. Why didn't they come and see us a single time in three
years, why did they (and why do they continue to) hide the real
levels of radioactivity in our district?'

Although representatives of the regional department of health
and the Ukrainian State Committee for Hydrology and
Meteorology were present in the room, none of them gave clear
answers to the questions put by the deputies. The deputy Health
Minister of the Ukraine, Yuri Spizhenko, declared categorically:
'... I can't talk about the ecological situation in the region, because
I was not prepared for such a question.' Three years after the
disaster, Spizhenko, who was actually the head of the health
department in Zhitomir region at the time of the catastrophe,
proposed 'the setting up of an objective commission comprising

doctors, and representatives from the authorities and the local press, who could publicise the work and objectivity of the facts presented by this commission.' What a strange proposal. Who would set up this commission? Perhaps a tractor driver from the Mayak collective farm? Or the leader of the district soviet? It was easy to see how the deputy minister 'was not prepared'…

Someone in the hall remarked: 'We get the impression that you aren't prepared to answer the proposals being made today, and that you have no proposals yourself for improving the ecological situation. You only visited this region as deputy minister of health to show yourself in a good light.' To which Yuri Spizhenko replied with dignity: 'It is not for you to make such pronouncements.'

A short while later, Deputy Minister Spizhenko took over the post of Minister. And it was in this role that he gave the following government-approved reply to my request which was accompanied by a collective letter from the village of Ostapi in Lugini district: 'At the present time, all files pertaining to the need to allocate special advantages to the population, especially to that of the villages of Malakhovka, Moshchanitsa, and Ostapi in Lugini district, Zhitomir region, are being examined by the government of the republic.'

This reply surprised me. Had the honourable minister read my letter? Had he heard what had been said in the session of the Lugini district soviet? What advantages for Moshchanitsa and Malakhovka was he talking about, as they already benefited from all the available advantages: 'coffin allowance' and the 25 per cent income supplement? It could only mean one thing: why throw yet more millions of roubles down the drain in the villages 'under strict control'? The people wanted to be evacuated to safe regions!

Or had the minister only sent this reply to show that they were looking into the case?

Which is worse, radioactivity, or our bureaucratic fortresses which destroy the human person?

Rudnia-Radovelskaya, in Ovruch district. The village was divided into two camps. Some wanted to leave, others said: where can we go? But what was certain was, they had to go.

In the new villages nobody planted trees. Think about it.

It is terrible for the people of all these villages to leave and abandon everything. Their hearts break at the thought, and they are like birds in cages, whether it be at Narodichi, Moshchanitsa, Polyessko, or elsewhere.

TEN

The forty secret protocols of the wise men of the Kremlin

I WAS a member of the parliamentary commission created by the Supreme Soviet of the USSR to look into the actions of those in positions of responsibility in the aftermath of the Chernobyl accident. According to its statutes, the commission had the power to ask for and obtain any document. Nearly all the administrations, the Ministry of Health, the Ministry of Defence, the State Committee for Hydrology and Meteorology, supplied us, albeit reluctantly, with secret documents. Only the Politburo of the Communist Party of the USSR did not respond to the official requests. I am convinced that we would never have received these documents if it had not been for the failed coup of August 1991.

After Boris Yeltsin's decree outlawing the Communist Party, its archives were opened and we at last received the secret protocols of the meetings of the Politburo's operational group which dealt with matters arising from the Chernobyl accident and the clean-up, which was headed by Nikolai Rizhkov. But despite the experts' requests to the parliamentary photocopying office for just one copy, they always met with refusal. And this was when the Communist Party no longer existed!

Reading through these unique documents, it occurred to me that the most dangerous isotope to escape from the mouth of the reactor did not appear on the periodic table. It was not 'Cs-137' (the isotope of Caesium). It was 'Lie-86'. A lie as global as the disaster itself.

Lie number 1:
About the victims of the radiation

The first meeting of the Politburo's operational group was held on 29 April 1986. By mid-May, it was meeting daily. (Compare this with the repeated claims, that we were told for years, that the leaders did not know what was happening. Recently still, in a television interview, Nikolai Rizhkov almost swore that at that time 'we did not know much'.)

As from 4 May, a flood of information reached the group about people who had been admitted to hospital.

SECRET. PROTOCOL NO. 5, 4 MAY 1986
Those attending: N. Rizhkov, E. Ligachev, V. Vorotnikov, V. Chebrikov, members of the Politburo, V. Dolgikh, S. Sokolov, candidates for membership of the Politburo, A. Yakovlyev, secretary of the Central Committee, A. Vlasov, Minister of the Interior.
... It is relevant to take into consideration the fact that on 4 May, 1,882 people were treated in hospital. The total number of people treated reached 38,000.
204 people were discovered to have been affected to greater or lesser degrees by irradiation syndrome, of whom 64 were children. 18 are in a serious condition.

SECRET. PROTOCOL NO. 7, 6 MAY 1986
Those attending: V. Ligachev, V. Chebrikov, members of the Politburo, V. Dolgikh, candidate for membership of the Politburo, A. Yakovlyev, secretary of the Central Committee.
... To take into consideration the communication from Comrade Shchepine [first Deputy Minister of Health of the USSR] according to which on 6 May, the number of people treated in hospital rose to 3,454; among these, 2,609 were admitted, of whom 471 were children. According to more precise figures, the number of people affected by irradiation syndrome is 367 people, of whom 19 are children. Of these, 34 are in a serious condition. One hundred and seventy nine people have been admitted to six Moscow hospitals, of whom two are children.

SECRET. PROTOCOL NO. 8, 7 MAY 1986

Those taking part in the meeting: M. Gorbachev, Secretary-General of the Central Committee of the Communist Party of the Soviet Union, N. Rizhkov, E. Ligachev, V. Vorotnikov, V. Chebrikov, members of the Politburo, V. Dolgikh, candidate for membership of the Politburo, A. Vlasov, Minister of the Interior of the USSR.

... In one day, the list of people treated in hospital rose by 1,821. By 10 o'clock on 7 May the number of people admitted to hospital had reached 4,301, of whom 1,351 were children. In 520 of these, irradiation syndrome was diagnosed, including people working for the Ministry of the Interior of the USSR. The number of people whose condition is serious is 34.

SECRET. PROTOCOL NO. 12, 12 MAY 1986

... During the past day, 2,703 more people were treated in hospitals, mostly in Byelorussia. 10,198 people were admitted to hospital for observation or treatment, of whom 345 showed symptoms of irradiation syndrome. Among these were 35 children.

How can we compare this secret information with the obstinate silence of the media? Were there two versions of the truth, one for the patricians and one for the slaves? In Protocol no. 21 of 4 June 1986, under 'Directives to people needing to participate in press conferences for Soviet and foreign journalists', we read: 'In order to resolve the question of responsibility, certain parameters have been established. Up to the present, everyone who went to a health centre was examined. A form of symptom of irradiation syndrome has been diagnosed in 187 people (all members of staff at the power station). Twenty-four of them have since died (two perished at the moment of the accident). The diagnosis of irradiation syndrome has not been confirmed in the people who have been treated in hospital, including the children.'

No doubt, the wider the radioactivity spread, the better the health of Soviet citizens became. The Ukrainian Minister of Health, A. Romanyenko, still claimed several years after the disaster, at the May 1989 plenary session of the Central Committee of the

Communist Party of the Ukraine: 'I can say in all responsibility that apart from those people who have fallen ill, that is 209 people, there is now nobody suffering from any illness resulting from radioactivity.'

We can discover the secret of such declarations by consulting the documents of the operational group. This is the miracle which allowed millions of people who had been exposed to radiation to regain their health:

> SECRET. PROTOCOL NO. 9, 8 MAY 1986
> ... The Ministry of Health of the USSR has adopted new levels of radiation which can be tolerated by the population, ten times higher than the former levels (cf. attached documents). In certain cases, these levels can be multiplied by 50.

By way of explanation, these levels are five times higher than those permitted for people working in the engine room of a nuclear power station. An addendum to the protocol follows: 'Thus we can ensure the continued safety and health of people of all ages, even if the ambient level of radioactivity stays the same for two and a half years.' These levels were even applied to pregnant women and children. The secret medical conclusion drawn after consulting documents provided by the State Committee for Hydrology and Meteorology was signed by the Deputy Minister of Health of the USSR, Y. Sedunov. In this way, thousands of our fellow-citizens were instantaneously cured on 8 May 1986 without treatment or medication (for the sake of efficiency, simplicity and the 'scientific character' of the method, one might wonder, in view of the difficulties we are currently experiencing with medical supplies and equipment and hospital beds, whether it would not be desirable to decree, for example, that as from 1 May of the current year, the normal body temperature should not be 36.6 degrees but, for instance, 38 or 'in special cases' 39. Thus there would be no more illness).

A few years after the catastrophe, Academician Iline himself, the father of the well-known '35 rems for 70 years' thesis, was forced to recognise at a parliamentary hearing that the figure of 166,000 people evacuated must be multiplied by ten. 'Society must weigh up the *risks and benefits* [my emphasis] of such an operation.' When I heard this speech, I asked myself who was saying it, a doctor who must revere all life, or a miserly accountant clicking his abacus: a life here, a life there. But at the end, the academician himself had been forced to recognise: 'one million six hundred thousand children have been exposed to worrying doses of radiation, and we must decide what steps to take.' Note that these doses were calculated according to official figures concocted under the shelter of the 'secret' label affixed by the Central Committee. But from the point of view of the moral imperative which considers every victim to be a sin in civilised countries, by how many times should we multiply the doses?

Lie number 2:
That 'clean' products grow on radioactive land

SECRET. PROTOCOL NO. 32, 22 AUGUST 1986
… To take into consideration the communication of Comrade V. Murakhovskiy (appended) according to which … recommendations and measures have been prepared on the method of carrying out agricultural work on land contaminated to varying degrees by isotopes with a long half-life.

The wise men of the Kremlin who prepared these protocols could not help but know that cows give radioactive milk even if pastured on land where the level of caesium-137 is 'only' one curie per square kilometre(!).

… To consider it desirable to include meat with a higher than normal level of radioactive matter in State stocks destined for conservation, and equally in those destined for sale during the current year.

SECRET. APPENDIX TO POINT 10 OF PROTOCOL NO. 32

... Part of the meat produced in the area situated in the path of the fallout from the Chernobyl reactor contains quantities of radioactive matter higher than permitted levels. At the present time, freezers in several regions of Byelorussia, Ukraine and the Russian Federation contain about 10,000 tonnes of meat with degrees of contamination from 1.1 microcuries per kilogram (1.1 10^{-7} Ci/kg) to 1.0 microcuries per kilogram (1.0 10^{-6}) and from August to December, another 30,000 tonnes of meat with the same characteristics arrived.

In order to avoid the accumulation of large amounts of radioactive matter in people's bodies as a result of eating contaminated food, the Minister of Health of the USSR recommends *distributing the contaminated meat as widely as possible in the country* [my emphasis] and using it to make sausages, preserved meat, and meat products, in a proportion of one to ten with normal meat. In order to do this it will be necessary to process it in factories in most areas of the Russian Federation (except Moscow), Moldavia, and the republics of Transcaucasus, the Baltic States, Kazakhstan, and Central Asia. Signed: The Chair of the State Committee for Food and Agriculture of the USSR, V. Murakhovskiy.

APPENDIX TO PROTOCOL NO. 32, POINT 11:

On the use of milk in certain regions of Byelorussia and the Russian Federation by means of raising the permitted levels of radioactive matter.

As from 1 August a new permitted level of radioactivity in milk came into force throughout all the territories of the USSR, equal to 10^{-8} curies per litre [in "clean" milk the level is 10^{-12}]. Nevertheless, in certain districts in certain regions in Byelorussia, some of the milk received contains radioactive matter at a level of 10^{-7} curies per litre, and cannot be stabilised at the permitted levels, which complicates milk supplies in these areas.

Having taken these figures into account, I authorise the postponement of the date for the introduction of the new levels until 1 November 1986... Milk produced in these regions must not be exported. Signed M. Burgasov...

I have to add that according to Professor Burlakova, a highly placed personage has declared: 'Thanks to the raising of the temporarily permissible levels, the state has saved 1.7 billion roubles!'

It was only five years later, after numerous requests by members of the Congress of People's Deputies of the USSR, that the Federal Prosecutor's office finally opened judicial procedures on the sale of contaminated products. This is the statement by the Deputy Prosecutor-General of the USSR, V. Andreyev:

> During the period 1986-1989, 47,500 tonnes of meat and 2 million tonnes of milk with higher than permitted levels of radioactivity were produced in the areas indicated. Byelorussia alone exported 15,000 tonnes of contaminated meat from its territorries. The circumstances mentioned led to contamination of food products with radioactive matter in practically the whole country, and may have a negative influence on the health of the population.

On the official authorisation of the Council of Ministers of the Russian Federation, in 1989 contaminated meat from the regions of Bryansk, Mogilev, Kiev and Zhitomir was sent to several regions of the Russian Federation and to the autonomous republics in Chuvashye and Komi.

The Soviet Union has broken up. There is no more Prosecutor-General of the USSR. Even in Bulgaria, a lawsuit has already been brought against people hiding information on radioactivity. But here, where a planetary catastrophe happened, the guilty have not been found, neither under the rule of the Party elite who called for 'reinforcing the propaganda measures to unmask the lies and inventions of the bourgeois information sources and secret services on the events at the Chernobyl nuclear power station', nor under the democrats: the prosecutors of the independent states keep silent.

Lie number 3:
What they told the press

Obviously, the press was not admitted to the meetings of the operational group. A single time, on 26 May (Protocol no. 18), the editors-in-chief of 'Central' newspapers were invited. They were given the following mandate: 'To focus attention on the measures taken by the Central Committee of the Communist Party of the USSR and the government to maintain the living and working conditions of the evacuated populations and to deal with the effects of the accident, widely reflecting the active participation of the workers in the carrying out of these measures'.

At nearly all the meetings a statement by somebody to the press, television, or at a press conference was examined. All these texts were approved and a definite publication date indicated.

SECRET. PROTOCOL NO. 9, 8 MAY 1986.
... 4. Concerning the television appearance of Comrades A. Vorobyev and E. Gogine. Taking into account the improved situation at the Chernobyl nuclear power station, it is considered desirable not to go ahead with this interview. 6. Concerning the TASS communiqué on the restrictions on imports from the USSR in several European countries. To approve the text of this communiqué and publish it in the press after a special decision.

SECRET. PROTOCOL NO. 5, 4 MAY 1986.
... To approve the text of the TASS communiqué. To postpone the publication of the communiqué from the Council of Ministers until 5 May.

It is interesting to note that neither these texts nor their authors are given in the protocols. As if they were afraid of leaving any proof.

SECRET. PROTOCOL NO. 1, 29 APRIL 1986.
... 10. Concerning the government communiqués. To approve the

text of the government communiqué for publication in the press. To approve the text of information supplied to the leaders of certain capitalist countries on the accident at the Chernobyl nuclear power station and the measures taken to deal with the consequences. To approve the text of the communiqué to the leaders of certain socialist countries on the operation to deal with the consequences of the accident at the Chernobyl power station.

Isn't it remarkable: one set of information for internal use, or rather disinformation, another for our brothers in the socialist camp, and a third for the 'evil' capitalists?

SECRET. PROTOCOL NO. 7, 6 MAY 1986.
... To accept the proposal of the State Committee for Hydrology and Meteorology on the need to inform the IAEA regularly of radiation levels in the regions surrounding the Chernobyl nuclear power station. To examine in advance all information destined for the IAEA at meetings of the operational group... To accept the proposal of the Ministry of Health of the USSR on the need to publish figures on the number and the condition of patients being treated at a Moscow hospital, *taking into account that there are Americans working at this hospital* [my emphasis].

SECRET. PROTOCOL NO. 3, 1 MAY 1986.
... To send a group of Soviet journalists to the region surrounding the Chernobyl power station, in order to prepare materials destined for the press and television demonstrating normal activities in these regions.

In other words, the article had virtually been written already.

The attempt by the special correspondent from *Izvestia* in Byelorussia, N. Matukovskiy, to attract the attention of the high assembly failed.

SECRET. APPENDIX TO PROTOCOL NO. 28
For the attention of telex operators. Do not show this telegram to anyone except the editor-in-chief. Destroy the copy... Information: I am drawing to your attention the fact that the

radioactivity situation has become slightly complicated in Byelorussia. We have discovered radioactive contamination in several districts of Mogilev, where the level is much higher than in the districts mentioned in our articles. According to all medical advice, residence in these areas constitutes a great risk to human life... I am communicating this to you by telex because telephone conversations on this subject are categorically forbidden. 8 July 1986. N. Matukovskiy.

The correspondent's alarmed telegram was transmitted to the operational group. After it had been discussed, it was decided 'to ask the State Committee for Hydrology and Meteorology (Comrade Izrael), the Ministry of Health of the USSR (Comrade Burenkov) and the USSR Academy of Science (Comrade Alexandrov), together with the Byelorussian Council of Ministers (Comrade Kovalyev), to check the radioactivity situation in the regions mentioned in the attached communiqué and the communicate the results to the operational group before 20 July.'

This disagreeable topic was mentioned no more during that session. And nobody took any notice of the results...

And this is how they prepared for a press conference for Soviet and foreign journalists.

SECRET. 4 JUNE 1986
... Appendix to Protocol no. 21. Directives for information given to the press conference on the main questions linked to the causes of, and progress in dealing with the consequences of, the accident in Block 4 of the Chernobyl power station... 2. When giving information on the progress of the clearing-up operation: demonstrate the efficient execution of large-scale technical and organisational measures which have no parallel in practice worldwide, to deal with the consequences of the accident and to prevent harm being caused by radioactivity; note the high level of mass heroism in the carrying out of the aforementioned work. Explain the large-scale measures taken to ensure the safety of the population, noting in particular the care taken of people in the contaminated areas... 4. Indicate the unjust character of the claims and judgements made both by certain prominent personages

and by the press from certain western countries, which speak of ecological and material damage caused by the spread of small quantities of radioactive matter carried by air from the Chernobyl area.

'Small quantities' means 300 Hiroshima bombs' worth of caesium-137 alone. And the 'insignificant damage' means, according to independent experts, damage worth 180-200 billion roubles a year up to the year 2000 at 1989 prices. And that is not counting the losses linked to the ill-health of thousands of people.

I could continue like this for a long time. **Lie number 4**, on the participation of the army in the clear-up operation. **Lie number 5**, on the founding of Slavutich, a new town built for the power station workers in a contaminated zone. **Lie number 6**, on the choice of senior executives and 'political education' at the Chernobyl reactor after the accident. And so on. And so on.

These new secret documents reveal ancient truths: each time it tries to maintain itself, the System inevitably has to do harm and hide its actions. Starting with the secret execution in the cellar of the Ipatyev house of children whose only crime was to have been born into the imperial family. Then it was the millions of us executed, sent to camps and psychiatric hospitals without trial; the bloody suppression of the Novocherkassk rebellion, the Afghanistan war, the tanks at Baku and Vilnius... Chernobyl, slow death by radioactivity, is part of this same list of crimes of the System against its own people, massacred methodically for decades like the mythical Gorgon Medusa who devoured her own children. The Gorgon could only be vanquished one way, by cutting off her head.

ELEVEN

'Our children are dying. Help!'

Letters from the high-radioactivity zone

'I am not yet thirty-two, and I have to go into hospital several times a year. My four children, the eldest of whom is twelve, are constantly sick too (weakness, pains in their joints, low haemoglobin counts, enlarged thyroid and lymphatic glands, headaches, stomach aches, nonstop throat infections). It's the same in all the families.

We want to live. We want our children to live and grow up healthy, and for them to have a future. Because of the indifference, hard-heartedness, and cruelty of those on whom our destiny and that of our children depends, we are condemned to the most terrible fate, which we well understand. The only ones who don't understand are the bureaucrats in their comfy armchairs.

They promise the people of Narodichi that they will evacuate at least a few villages, but in our district it is never mentioned. And for so many years we have been forced to eat and drink radioactivity, to breathe it in and just wait for our last hour. And all this in the land of the soviets, where it is always said (on the radio, in the newspapers, at school) that humanity is always the central priority!

It's not true! No-one cares about us. Who can we turn to? If I knew, I would write to the United Nations, because our local authorities, like the press, are as impotent as ourselves.

We pray you, we beg you to help us in our misfortune, to save our children!'

Valentina Nikolayevna Okhremchuk, mother of four small boys, and all the mothers of Olevsk district.

'We, the inhabitants of Maryanovka village, Narodichi district, Zhitomir region, call on you for help. The whole world has left us alone with our misfortune.

We shall never forget April 1986. Although three years have gone by, the Chernobyl accident worries us more and more. Its effects on our children's health are getting worse. Tears come to our eyes when we look at them, but we can't do anything to help them. it's easy to see that our children aren't like they were before. Where has their energy gone, their joy, their laughter? They are often ill. And it's not just isolated cases. More and more, we are eating the produce from our own gardens, although we know that we shouldn't. We have no choice. In the whole collective farm, the level of contamination in the milk is very high, several times higher than the permitted levels. There are no fruit and vegetables in the shop; and as for milk, we only get what hasn't been sold in the villages which get 'clean' products. These villages are three or four kilometres from ours.

Our village is not large. Practically all the people who live here work on the collective farm. There is no other work, so we don't earn much, sixty to seventy roubles on average. And there are families with three or four children.'

Signed by thirteen farmworkers from Maryanovka.

'Quite a few of the people from Mezhilesk have moved away, but most of us have stayed despite everything. We are sure that our State will not permit its workers to suffer. But here is the reason for this letter: at nearby villages—at Bazar, Golubievichi, Bolshye Minki and elsewhere—people get a

25 per cent income supplement, as well as 30 roubles per inhabitant. We don't know what the difference is between their situation and ours. The radiological laboratory came to our farm and when we spoke to the workers, we understood that the levels recorded by the laboratory were the same here as there.

To give concrete examples, we can say for definite that our sheep have already been taken away to neighbouring districts, because our farm is unusable. It was the same last year, it's the same this year. The level of radioactivity of our cows has also been measured, and it is very high, even in those which have been reared for meat; so we can't take them to the slaughterhouse.

Seventy per cent of our pre-school children have been diagnosed as having illness-causing thyroid problems. They have been prescribed a six-month treatment, and they are recommended not to drink milk from our cows, as well as only to eat "clean" food brought from elsewhere.

In our village there is a primary school. We don't know why, but a troop of soldiers came and dug up and carried away a layer of earth from by the school, and they put gravel down in its place. When people asked why they were doing it, they replied that there was a high level of radioactivity.

That is what led us to write in order to find a just solution to this problem. Because we work conscientiously on the farm and in the fields, and we continue to work, even if we do worry a lot about our children. We have been told that in time, things will get back to normal. We ask to be given an income supplement like in the neighbouring villages. Then we could buy "clean" products for our children.'

The workers of the villages of Mezhilesk and Osoka.
[Ten signatures]